THE ROYAL IRISH CONSTABULARY

D1603115

CLASSICS OF IRISH HISTORY
General Editor: Tom Garvin

Other titles in this series:

THE ROYAL IRISH CONSTABULARY

A HISTORY AND PERSONAL MEMOIR

Thomas Fennell
(R.I.C. NO. 41310)

edited by
Rosemary Fennell

UNIVERSITY COLLEGE DUBLIN PRESS
PREAS CHOLÁISTE OLLSCOILE BHAILE ÁTHA CLIATH

First published 2003 by University College Dublin Press
© The Estate of Thomas Fennell 2003
Introduction and notes © Rosemary Fennell 2003

ISBN 1 904558–00–3
ISSN 1383–6883

University College Dublin Press
Newman House, 86 St Stephen's Green
Dublin 2, Ireland
www.ucdpress.ie

All rights reserved. No part of this publication may be
reproduced, stored in a retrieval system, or transmitted
in any form or by any means, electronic, photocopying,
recording, or otherwise without the prior written
permission of the publisher.

Cataloguing in Publication data
available from the British Library

Typeset in Ireland in Baskerville by
Elaine Shiels, Bantry, Co. Cork
Printed on acid-free paper in Ireland
by ColourBooks, Dublin

CONTENTS

INTRODUCTION
Rosemary Fennell

Thomas Fennell was a member of the Royal Irish Constabulary, 1875–1905. He died in 1948 and, as an old man already in his late seventies, began his memoir and history of the Force in which he had served. It is clear from the text that he intended it for publication but it has had to wait for over fifty years since his death for this ambition to be realised.

Despite the passage of time, there is much of interest in this memoir politically and socially. Not surprisingly, the agrarian agitation and reform of land tenure which dominated so much of the Irish political scene in the last quarter of the nineteenth century is much in evidence (see especially chapters 4, 8, 12, 13, and 15). As the police force, the R.I.C. was caught squarely in the middle and their personal feelings must have often been in conflict with their duties. It should never be forgotten that a very high proportion of the rank and file came from farming backgrounds and that admission to the Force was seen as a means of advancement for young men with a modicum of education and ambition.

The agrarian agitation was a turning point which changed the pace of policing and altered the role of the R.I.C. in many ways. Prior to that, as Fennell describes: "A police force was required in every country, and what objection could there be to join the Irish police, more than any other police force?" (chapter 1, "Organisation and recruiting"). With the start of the Land War, the R.I.C. found itself sucked into a much more openly political position. It was only after serving for some time in the Force that the men began to see an agenda other than that of the preservation of peace and order. But, by that time, they had been drawn deeply into the system, were probably married and with families.

In a sense, the Land War was a dress rehearsal for the equally uncomfortable role which the R.I.C. was to play in the War of Independence. In both, the Force had to contend with "special assistance" foisted on it by the respective governments of the day. During the Land War, army reservists were provided to help the police with protection duties. The R.I.C. objected to these men wearing the same uniform and so it was modified by white facings. These auxiliaries were not a success: "they failed absolutely to live under the rigid discipline of the R.I.C. and were dismissed one after another" (see chapter 12). This experience was a foretaste of the confusion of the R.I.C. with the Black and Tans and the Auxiliaries—dealt with at passionate length in the Addendum. Interestingly, Fennell maintains that during the Land War the population at large understood that the police were carrying out work which they found distasteful and he contrasts this with the more hostile situation in the War of Independence. He also refers to the recognition Michael Davitt gave to the R.I.C. as a source of information for the Land League (see chapter 13)— the parallels with Michael Collins's use of the R.I.C. is obvious.

One small personal regret I have in Fennell's treatment of the agrarian agitation is that his valiant attempt at even-handedness and objectivity masks the reality of what he must have witnessed. As a young member of the Force his first posting was to Mayo at the end of 1875 and he remained there for nearly eight years. When, in chapter 12, he describes Michael Davitt "standing on the ruins of the home of his childhood from which his family had been evicted, [calling] upon the people to band themselves together to overthrow the system which had inflicted on them such heartless tyranny and injury", was he recalling what he himself had seen and heard?

Another important political issue covered by this memoir is the role of the R.I.C. as an instrument of repression. Fennell's position on this is somewhat ambiguous but he vehemently takes to task both Dorothy McArdle and Piaras Beaslai for their anti-R.I.C. views—particularly the assertion that the R.I.C. was engaged in espionage on behalf of the State. In this regard, Fennell makes two very pertinent points: that the R.I.C. provided no advance warning of the Rising of 1916 and that the spying of certain members was on behalf of Michael Collins! (See especially the Addendum.)

This Addendum is a remarkable *tour de force* written by a very old man in defence of the integrity of the R.I.C. during the War of Independence. He castigates many of the actions taken against them—particularly the ambushing of foot patrols on country roads—and he singles out for special criticism the very first assassinations at Soloheadbeg in Tipperary. He is contemptuous of the attacks which continued to take place during the Truce by people whom he saw as climbing on the Republican bandwagon when it was safe to do so. Again there is a parallel with the land agitation where "people of no account became local leaders and platform spouters, self being the chief idea at the back of their minds" (p. 106). In contrast, he has nothing but praise for members of the R.I.C. who acted humanely and who stuck to their principles. He recounts with pride the famous incident at Listowel in 1920 when Constable Jeremiah Mee and fourteen of his colleagues resigned rather than carry out unjust orders (p. 109).

While defending the R.I.C. vigorously against the accusation of spying, Fennell frequently acknowledges that the police were an instrument of support for the political status quo and in particular the position of the Ascendancy and the landowning class. This comes across very clearly in chapter 11 on the administration of the law. He also recognised that, in a sense, there was absolutely no need to indulge in repressive behaviour, as the day-to-day activities of a force dispersed throughout the countryside in small groups meant that they knew everything about everybody in the area and were therefore a mine of information (see chapter 2, "Strength and distribution of the force"). Added to this, its organisation was highly bureaucratic with a detailed system of upward reporting—a good insight to this can be found in chapter 9, "Correspondence".

Socially, the R.I.C. reflected the Ireland of the nineteenth century. The officer class was drawn very largely from the Protestant Ascendancy; the rank and file were from a rural background, predominantly though not exclusively Roman Catholic. Religious tensions there most certainly were as can be seen in chapter 10, "Bigotry". However, on a day-to-day basis in a highly disciplined and professional body, people held their tongue and got on with the job in hand. The major exception was in relation to promotion—particularly to the officer class (see especially chapter 7, "Promotion"). In 1885, Sir Andrew Reed was appointed Inspector General of the R.I.C. Uniquely he was a member of the Force, not a British import, having entered as an officer cadet and worked his way up. He was a reformer in every respect, not least in his attempts to open up promotions to Catholics (see especially chapters 3 and 7). In this he faced considerable opposition and found his own position undermined. Indeed, after his retirement, some of his promotion reforms were watered down. It is quite clear from the memoir that Fennell had a very high regard for Reed who was "policeman's policeman" who understood the Force in a way no outsider could.

In considering the R.I.C. in the context of Irish society, one of the most interesting chapters of the memoir is chapter 13, on how service affected the men. Here Fennell confronts the issue of a force seen as an arm of the State which yet is deeply rooted in the society from which its members were recruited. They were popular—much sought after as marriage partners—and there was never any difficulty in finding an ample supply of recruits, even during the Land War. He raises the question of whether members should have resigned during the agrarian agitation, thereby hastening its resolution and answers his own question by pointing out the alternative: "Gaps made by individual resignations could have been filled by auxiliaries of one sort of another—Englishmen, ex-soldiers, Orangemen— and would these have been an improvement on the R.I.C.?"

One very telling aspect of the R.I.C.'s position in Irish society was the sheer number of the Force. Ireland was heavily policed and, given that the majority of the men married and had families, they comprised a sizeable group in that society. Taking the men and their dependents together, Fennell puts it at up to half a million over the lifetime of the Force. One small illustration of this is that, when Fennell's first wife died in 1905, the obituaries in the Sligo newspapers mentioned among the mourners her brother-in-law and a cousin, both sergeants in the R.I.C. I suspect that there is hardly anyone in Ireland who does not have somewhere in their family tree a member of the R.I.C. or the D.M.P. (Dublin Metropolitan Police).

Who was Thomas Fennell? This is not an easy question to answer, given the paucity of primary family historical sources in Ireland and the fallibility of family folklore. Thomas was born in 1857 in Creagh, Castledermot, County Derry—despite family folklore that he was born in County Antrim. His police record (reproduced in appendix 1) gives two counties of origin—Londonderry and Antrim. Presumably the latter is included because, as a teenager, Thomas moved to Antrim in search of work. (In his police record, his occupation at entry is given as "labourer".) Certainly, his recommendation as a candidate for entry to the Force was provided by District Inspector Wray who, at the time, was in charge of the Antrim Town District of County Antrim.

Thomas was said to be the son of a farmer but neither the Griffith Valuation nor the "Owners of land of 1 acre and upwards" (HMSO, 1876) lists the father as owning any land. This suggests he was either a tenant farmer or even a farm worker; it is impossible to tell. According to one family source, Thomas had a brother who emigrated to Australia but no amount of searching in Australian records has provided any evidence of this.

Again, according to family folklore, Thomas is said to have been poorly educated in a formal sense, yet he was capable of joining the police at an early age and of subsequently passing examinations for promotion firstly to Sergeant and then to Head Constable. He also took the examinations for promotion to District Inspector. If he was self-taught he did an excellent job, as his style of writing in the memoir bears witness. It was also reported in the *Sligo Independent* (10 November 1900) that "Head Constable Thomas Fennell, of Sligo, is the author of a capital little work on company drill, which has just been issued by the publishers. The book should prove a great help to all those interested in drill and desirous of obtaining a sound knowledge of its intricacies." I have not been able to trace a copy of this book.

His obituaries (reproduced in appendix 2) refer to him writing articles for journals—no one in the family can throw light on this activity. Were they tips for the amateur gardener or political polemic? One tantalising feature of the Addendum, where he takes McArdle and Beaslai to task for misrepresentation of the role of the R.I.C., is that he cites which edition of McArdle's *Irish Republic* he was using and twice quotes the actual page numbers—an attention to detail and source referencing which one might not have expected from someone with no training or experience in research—particularly very late in life.

So Thomas's origins are obscure and his education questionable; a further puzzle arises over his age at entry to the police: 18 years. The normal minimum was 19 and it was usually only if a boy's father or other close relative was already in the R.I.C. (or was an R.I.C. pensioner) that a lower age was acceptable. There is no evidence in the R.I.C. records that such a family member existed. However, as he was within ten days of his nineteenth birthday when he joined the Force, it is likely that the age rule was relaxed in his case.

There are two stories as to why Thomas resigned on pension from the R.I.C. in May 1905 at the age of 48. One is that, having passed his written examinations for promotion to

District Inspector (which according to a notice in the *Sligo Independent* he took in 1901), he was subsequently not promoted, having hit a glass ceiling on grounds of religion. The other version is that he turned down the promotion on the grounds that he did not have the financial wherewithal to hold the D.I. rank in a fitting manner. Frankly, this latter view is hard to match to the man. Why sit the examinations if you do not intend to take the promotion? He was clearly an ambitious man and his memoir returns again and again to the question of discrimination within the Force and in particular to the paucity of openings for Catholic head constables to move into the officer rank. There is a touch of bitterness in his references to the dying days of the R.I.C. when promotions were freely available. A look at the relevant years in the R.I.C. records bears this out with a flurry of promotions of Catholics to D.I. level.

Thomas Fennell was my grandfather. He died when I was ten but I never met him. As in so many Irish families, our closest contacts were with our mother's side of the family. I did not know of the existence of this memoir until the mid-1990s. When I read it I realised that my grandfather wrote it with the intention of having it published and I resolved to try to fulfil belatedly the wish of this old man who, despite the disappointment of his career ambition, clearly was immensely proud of the Force in which he served.

I should like to thank my cousin the late Pat Murphy who provided me with some of the folklore and with some wonderful photographs; my cousin Deirdre Murphy for having given me more family background, particularly as she hazily remembered our grandfather in Sligo towards the end of his life; my cousin Grainne Murphy Gregory for having lent me family photographs and the version of the memoir typed by her mother Lena. This helped me fill in some of the gaps in the other surviving version of the text; and my brother Desmond who drew my attention to the existence of the memoir in the first place. The help of the staff of the Registry of births, marriages and deaths in Dublin, the National Library of Ireland, the National Archives of Ireland, the UK Public Records Office at Kew, and Garda Jim Herlihy is gratefully acknowledged. And finally, my thanks to Professor Tom Garvin of University College Dublin who suggested an ideal vehicle for publishing the memoir and who encouraged me to write this Introduction and undertake the editorial work on the text.

As to that text, due to its chequered history no flawless version exists. I have made what minor corrections were possible and have checked names of persons and places, and dates where possible. All footnotes and text in square brackets have been added by me.

THE ROYAL IRISH CONSTABULARY

Thomas Fennell and Catherine McIntyre, married September 1886

CHAPTER ONE.

ORGANISATION AND RECRUITING.

I have often thought that it would be well if someone who had passed through the Royal Irish Constabulary would leave behind him a record of the conditions that prevailed in that Force.

For eighty years or more, that Force played an important part in the government of Ireland. Indeed, to write a complete history of the R.I.C. would be almost equivalent to writing Irish history for that period, for it was the organisation chiefly relied upon to enforce English rule in this country during those years. It should, therefore, be of interest to many, and perhaps of some advantage to future historians to have first-hand information of the organisation and rule in that service.

As no one has taken such a work in hand, I am now, at the eleventh hour, making the venture. After a good deal of consideration as to the plan I should adopt to place on record the knowledge I gained during thirty years of the system that fashioned that Force into a perfect machine for enforcing English rule in Ireland, I have decided on confining myself to a simple narrative, without any attempt at literary style, to which I am only too conscious I can lay no claim. Indeed, I feel that in a simple narrative I can best attain my purpose. I had the advantage of a varied experience in the Force, giving me a wide general knowledge of the service. I have only then to set down, as clearly as I can, what I have learned during the thirty years in that service. I feel the difficulty of arranging the order of the task before me, so as to avoid repetition and make my story clear to the reader; but this will not deter me.

After the failure of the 1798 Insurrection and the passage of
the Act of Union, Ireland lay prostrate in the dust and
remained wounded and broken during the first decade of the
nineteenth century. There seemed little hope that she would
ever again stand strong and erect, to continue the long struggle
she had waged to regain her freedom; fate seemed to have
sealed the lot of her people to absolute slavery. Yet, the spirit
of revolt lived on through the formation of secret societies,
chief of which was the White Boys, who aimed at the recovery
of the lands of which the people had been plundered, opposition to the collection of taxation, especially Church Tithes,
and resistance generally to English rule. The Whiteboys were
a daring and effective organisation. They moved in small
bodies through the country by night, levelling fences, tumbling
grain stacks, firing haggards, and generally making the lives of
Planters uncomfortable. As a means of recognition by one
another in their nightly operations, they wore bands of white:
hence "The Whiteboys". There is no doubt they were a for-
midable source of trouble to English rule for sixty years or
more, for in the reign of George III and that of William IV,
we find Acts of Parliament providing extreme penalties for
Whiteboyism. The offences set out in those enactments cover
a large and varied field of actions tending to intimidate and
cause fear among those against whom they were aimed. I
have read where someone has stated or written that to the
Whiteboys is chiefly due the credit for keeping alive the spirit
of resistance to English rule and passing it on to future generations, and will anyone, reading Irish history of the time, not
say that there is much truth in the assertion?

Grand juries and magistrates dispensed the law. The police
were nominated by the magistrates in Petty Sessions, and
appointed by the Lord Lieutenant and forthwith became constables without more ado. Chief Officers were appointed by
the Lord Lieutenant independently of the system of appointing
constables. Officers and constables might be appointed to a
County, Barony or Half Barony. The magistrates, who were of
the landlord class, controlled and issued orders to the police.

Mr. Peel, afterwards Sir Robert Peel, on his appointment as Chief Secretary in 1812, set about improving the police system and part of his remedial measures was the appointment of paid magistrates who were an amalgam of a justice of the peace and a police officer. They sat with the ordinary justices in Petty Sessions to guide them in their actions and took charge of the police when acting in bodies. These magistrates were continued by Acts 6 and 7 William IV, under which the entire police of the country were amalgamated under one authority in 1836. Previously, each province had a separate establishment ruled by a Chief Inspector.

A belief generally held was that the police of Peel's time as Chief Secretary was the same Force that came down from that time as the R.I.C. This was quite a mistaken view. The system of appointing and controlling the police remained unchanged during Peel's Chief Secretaryship of six years, and down to 1836, when the police of every county in Ireland were absorbed into a new organisation, under one central authority. Acts 6 and 7 Wm. IV provided that, on an appointed day, the police of every county—officers and men—should cease to hold office as such and were to become members of the new organisation without change of status, on first taking the following oath: "I, A.B. do swear that I will well and truly serve our Sovereign Lord, the King, in the office of (rank) without favour or affection, malice, or ill will, that I will see and cause His Majesty's peace to be kept and preserved, and that I will prevent, to the best of my power, all offences against the same, and, that whilst I shall hold the said office, I will, to the best of my skill and knowledge, discharge all the duties thereof in the execution of warrants and otherwise, faithfully according to law; and that I do not now belong, and that I will not, while I shall hold the said office, join, subscribe, or belong to any political society, whatsoever, unless the society of Freemasons."

The Lord Lieutenant was given power to appoint an Inspector General and other officers, and "to authorise the Inspector General to make rules and regulations to provide for one uniform system in the whole establishment of police in Ireland".

Some idea of the material that went to make up the police previous to 1836 may be gathered from the qualifications required of men for the new organisation. Here they are: "no person to be appointed chief or other constable unless he shall be of sound constitution, able-bodied and under the age of forty years, be able to read and write, and of good character for honesty, fidelity and activity". No provision for pensions appears to have existed in the police forces previous to 1836— nor even then. Men probably took up the job as a means of existence for the time, without intending to remain longer than suited them. At no time do they appear to have been an effective force. To cope with possible trouble yeomanry and military were called to their aid. The military quartered in small bodies all over the country was the principal force relied upon to keep in subjection the spirit of turbulence then coming to the surface.

Comparing the qualifications required by men admitted to the reorganised Force with those of R.I.C. recruits, it will be seen the great difference in the class of men that made up the amalgamated Force in 1836 with that of the R.I.C. And let it not be forgotten that previous to Catholic Emancipation, Catholics were not admitted into any of the police forces. Once an old police register came into the hands of the writer, and it was seen that men bearing Catholic names were registered as Protestants. No doubt the camouflage was not questioned, or else the men were of little worth—servants or hangers-on to those in authority. Even in 1836 when amalgamation of the various police bodies took place, under the rule of the celebrated Thomas Drummond, the new Force consisted of seven thousand men, five thousand of whom were Orangemen; the five Inspectors General and the County Inspectors were Protestants. Drummond insisted on the admission of Catholics to the police. "If you do not admit Catholics", he said, "you do not gain the confidence of the people".

Here, we have ample evidence that the oft-repeated assertion that the R.I.C. was created by Peel, on his arrival here as Chief Secretary in 1812, is not true. In 1840, under the rule of

Queen Victoria, the Depot in the Phoenix Park was formed, and from this event may the establishment of the R.I.C. be correctly stated. But anything that was considered demeaning and hurtful was picked up and thrown at the Force without question. One of the groundless—and what was thought was the most damaging of charges—was that they afforded protection to the collectors of Church Tithes. The police of that time were unable themselves to afford that protection, and were usually accompanied by yeomanry or military, or both. The need to collect this impost ceased when it was included in the rents paid to the landlords from 1838. In the collection of tax, especially Church Tithes, bodies of police and yeomanry were often employed to protect the bailiffs, and it was very essential to have a qualified responsible officer in command of those armed bodies. Already serious conflicts with loss of life had occurred, and the creation by Peel of stipendiary magistrates to have charge of armed parties on such occasions, as well as presiding at Petty Sessions to guide the magistrates in their actions, would seem to have been necessary at the time. This is the only scrap of evidence relied upon to support the allegation that Peel was the author of the R.I.C. and which for generations has been offensively flung at the Force as "Peelers".

From this digression, I shall now try and sketch the origin and development of the R.I.C. The Government had now to cope with not only agrarian discontent but with a revolutionary movement as well. A police force, armed and drilled as soldiers, was therefore conceived and, in 1840, the Depot in the Phoenix Park was established. A Reserve Force consisting of four Sub-Inspectors, four Head Constables, and two hundred Sergeants and Constables was stationed there for the purpose of speedily reinforcing the police in cases of sudden and extraordinary emergency. Here, recruits were drafted as in a military barracks before allocation to counties. Instruction in police duties, as well, formed part of their training. The chief officers consisted of an Inspector General, a Deputy, and one or two Assistant Inspectors General with their offices in Dublin Castle. There was also a Commandant of the Depot

who had quarters there. An army officer, of the rank of
Colonel, was always appointed Inspector General, except in
one instance when Sir Andrew Reed, an officer of the Force,
was appointed to that position in the middle 1880s.

Though nominally the R.I.C. may be said to date from
1836, yet, as a semi-military body, its existence dates more
accurately from the establishment of the Depot in 1840.
Dating then from 1840, the Force was trained as a military
police. The Depot differed nothing from a military barracks.
There, recruits were drilled as soldiers for six months or
more, until proficient in the use of arms and military movements. They were schooled in the elements of police duties.
The Force, therefore, became an important adjunct to the
military, as an army of occupation in the country. For many
years, it was officered exclusively by men of the Ascendancy
class. Though the rank and file were eighty per cent Catholic,
the officers with few exceptions were Protestant. These
entered as cadets after passing a qualifying examination. They
had first to obtain a nomination by the Lord Lieutenant, so
that care was taken to confine these appointments to the
desired class. They were principally the sons of broken down
gentlemen and clergymen, a few being Englishmen. After
years of agitation, a small proportion and eventually, from the
middle 1880s, half the appointments were made by the promotion of Head Constables. This made no practical change.
The Force had now been organised and disciplined for years
on stringent lines as an instrument in the hands of Dublin
Castle, which was virtually the Government, to be employed
in every eventuality to sustain landlordism and Castle rule in
Ireland. No officer or man would, therefore, act in a way, no
matter what his feelings were, that would even arouse suspicion
that he was not to be trusted as a faithful member. Indeed,
there was no need to fear that any officer or man, having any
regard for his position, would risk an attitude that would
endanger his outlook in the service. A code of discipline, of the
most rigid character, ordered the daily lives of officers and
men, so that in time they became drilled into the system,

outside of which they did not look, and the daily routine of their duties became part of their existence. Of the entire system I shall try to give fuller details as we proceed.

Up to the early seventies, men employed in the service were miserably paid, and only an inferior class joined it, many of them resigning after a short time. In 1874, the pay of a Constable on joining was increased to £1 a week, with uniform and small allowances for boots and other necessaries. After their training at the Depot, recruits were allocated to counties. From £1 a week, Constables reached the maximum rate of £70 per annum after twenty years' service, Sergeants around £86; and Head Constables, the highest non-commissioned rank, £96 with a maximum of £104 per annum. All were pensionable. From time to time, after periods of agitation small increases of pay, pensions, and allowances were made. To a country boy, having no outlook save emigration to another country, the R.I.C. offered a rather favourable alternative, and the authorities were able to rely on a constant supply of first class recruits. On application, recruits were classed first, second, and third; but it was only when the condition of things in the country necessitated an increase of the Force that even second class applicants were called.

Up to 1879, the country was comparatively quiet. There was no objection to young men joining the service. A police force was required in every country, and what objection could there be to join the Irish police, more than any other police force? Recruits, generally, were the sons of small farmers, with a sprinkling of policemen's sons. These boys had received the ordinary elementary education of the National Schools. They had reached the sixth or seventh standard, or perhaps not so far. They had no knowledge whatever of Irish history, nor had their parents, and were absolutely in the dark as to the purpose of this Force, beyond the preservation of peace and order, like every other police force; indeed it was only after years of service that they began to see the chief purpose of it. Young men went on thoughtlessly, year after year, having a much improved position in life, carrying out what seemed to them the ordinary duties of a police force, with plenty of time for leisure and amusement.

As I have stated, it was only after ten or twelve years that they began to see that this Force was specially organised and equipped to sustain landlordism and keep the people in subjection. No matter how distasteful it was, they had then in most cases reached a time when they were obliged to continue. By that time, most men had married and had rising families. Men should have seven years' service before permission to marry was officially granted. The period of pre-marriageable service was considered rather long but, on the whole, was a wise arrangement, as young men were liable to get married without making provision for the responsibility which marriage brings along. Otherwise the authorities encouraged marriage, as men were then held to the service, and were obliged to go on under all conditions, however disagreeable.

The Force, as stated, was recruited from the peasantry. The limits of age were 18 to 27; 20 to 22 would be the average at entry. Candidates should be at least 5 ft 9 inches high, with minimum chest measurement of 37 inches and in every respect found surgically fit. They were examined in reading and writing from dictation, and in elementary arithmetic, in the District Inspector's office. Their papers, with certificates of character from a clergyman and one or two from people of good standing, were forwarded to the Depot, where they were classed 1st, 2nd, 3rd, and called for training as required. The course of training at the Depot was somewhat strenuous, especially in its early stages, but in no way an overtax on youthful joints and muscles. Dublin was a gay city and Phoenix Park, in which the Depot was situated, a beautiful resort. Outside training hours, recruits had perfect freedom to move through the city and Park, and enjoy the outings. The city was garrisoned by various branches of the army, splashing the street and environments with flashing uniforms, and with bands and bugles contributing to the joy of life. On the whole, the R.I.C. recruits coming up from various provinces found an entirely new and enjoyable life at the Depot.

Nor was there anything in the course of training to which exception could be taken. The Depot was a replica of any military barracks and the men were drilled as soldiers, some of the instructors being ex-military men. At one time, there was a small cavalry unit attached to the Force, and the officer in command had always been a Sergeant Major, appointed from a cavalry regiment, and given commissioned rank in this branch. In addition to military training, recruits were schooled in elementary police duties, but there was nothing in the entire course of training that was in any way repugnant or distasteful. Indeed, instead, the course should have been an advantage to boys coming up from the country, who had never received any training in cleanliness or orderly habits and, in most instances, were rough awkward boys whose knowledge of the world did not extend outside the district in which they had been reared. The drill instructors indulged to some extent in sarcasm and abuse, as in the army, in knocking off the rough corners in the moulding of recruits into shape, such as, "heads up; remember you are not now in the bog with the donkey and creels"; but that did not hurt them and, on the whole, they saw or heard nothing that was not to the advantage of any young man.

On Saturdays, on which there was no drill, the sergeant major paraded the Depot reserves, men and recruits, and lectured them on the course of conduct they were expected to follow. He was particularly severe on any of the older members giving a bad example to the recruits. In every one of his lectures he warned the recruits to avoid bad company, dwelling emphatically on the forcible old maxim "tell me your company, and I'll tell you what you are". I think I see him now, moving to and fro in the hollow square, dealing out fatherly advice to us boys, about to start on that career of which we knew so little. A splendid old type was Sergeant Major Preston, remembered by few today. In the schoolroom as well, the chief instructor, a kindly old gentleman, known as "Old Pro"—because he frequently warned the recruits that they were there only on probation and it was up to them to attend to their instructions—frequently lectured them on the need for good conduct and not to forget their people at home, but to help them by sending them money if needed and, especially, not to forget their sisters at "Set Times".

The great majority of the men were Catholic. The parade for Divine Service on Sundays was a thing to be remembered. Phibsboro was the church we attended in my time and the column, as it moved along the North Circular Road, and filed into the beautiful church, the body of which was reserved for our accommodation, made an indelible impression on our young minds.

In due course we were sent out to counties to fill vacancies and it was only then our practical education as policemen commenced. For a considerable time we were accompanied on duty by some of the older hands and not allowed to act on our own account until we had gained sufficient experience. Much depended on the place we were first stationed, but it was only after about five years that a young constable had gained sufficient experience to enable him to act independently with safety to himself and the public in the efficient discharge of the many duties he was called on to perform. Previous to the long agrarian troubles commencing in 1879, the duties of the police were of the ordinary routine nature and, as people had settled down to conditions of life in the country, the police moved freely among them and were very popular.

The agrarian struggle brought them more or less into conflict with the people and to some extent caused a change of feeling towards them. Still, they were never at any time up to the 1920 Troubles unpopular with the general public. The people realised that the duties the police were obliged to carry out during the Land War were most distasteful to them as well as heaping upon them loads of work and responsibility. The revolutionary struggle brought the police into violent conflict with the revolutionists and a wide gulf, for the time, between them and the majority of the people resulted. But the trouble was not of their making and many things to their credit happened during that time, which are referred to elsewhere. The establishment of a Parliament in Dublin for twenty-six counties and one in Belfast for six counties under the Treaty of 1921 led to demobilisation of the R.I.C. and the creation of a separate police force for each area.

CHAPTER TWO.

STRENGTH AND DISTRIBUTION OF THE FORCE.

The nominal strength of the Force was ten thousand of all ranks but in troubled periods this number was increased as required. With the Headquarters staff in Dublin, there was an Inspector in charge of each county. Cork, Galway and Tipperary were each divided into two ridings with an Inspector in each riding. Each county was divided into four or five districts according to size of the county, with a District (formerly titled Sub) Inspector in charge of each, and again, each district into sub-districts, with a Sergeant in charge of each. The chief town of each county was usually Headquarters of the County, and the smaller towns those of the districts. A Sergeant and four or five Constables were quartered in villages or other positions in each sub-district. County Headquarters consisted of a County Inspector, District Inspector, Head Constable—next grade to District Inspector—three or four Sergeants, and from fifteen to twenty Constables; District Headquarters consisted of a District Inspector, Head Constable, two or three Sergeants, and about ten Constables; Sub-Districts consisted of a Sergeant and four or five Constables. Thus the Force was distributed all over the country under one Code of Regulations.

Chief of the Instructions was to acquire a good local knowledge of the people, their condition of life, their relations through marriage or otherwise, how they were disposed towards one another, their political views, and every circumstance that would contribute to a complete knowledge of the lives of the people. A friendly intercourse was to be cultivated, so as to become familiar with the persons and habits of every individual in each district. A householder's register was kept at every station, showing the names and ages of everyone in each family and their relationship to one another. There was also a list of suspects kept. That list contained the names of individuals likely to be disposed to commit certain crimes. These persons were not always of bad character but often men whose attitude towards the Government was such that in political or agrarian matters they were likely to commit acts which, for the time, were illegal. The entire system could be regarded only as one of complete espionage, keeping the people continually under surveillance, so as to enable the police at all times, not only to cope with ordinary criminals, but to carry out government instructions in political and agrarian conflicts with success. On Inspections, the general knowledge of the men as to these instructions was tested.

Though appearing as a means only of coping with ordinary crime, the system of surveillance was devised specially to keep under observation political and agrarian movements. The people, generally, were peaceable and well disposed, yet the police Instructions were to the effect that the majority of them were [. . . text missing . . .] of a general character, and supposed to be carried out without creating suspicion. In the absence of definite orders, general Instructions especially if not needed were easily got over and, except to enable them to answer questions on Inspections, they gave the police very little concern; they had ample opportunities of gaining a knowledge of the people without prying into the privacy of their lives, and especially avoiding acting in a way that might be regarded as a hurtful intrusion. Of course, direct orders on any duties which had to be recorded in the books of the station had to be carried out, if men were to avoid the risk of getting into trouble themselves. But if free to use their own discretion, regulations and instructions generally got the go-by in matters where they were evidently needless.

Dublin Castle was the seat of Government, and here were the offices of the Chief Secretary, R.I.C. and other departments. These offices were manned for generations by permanent officials of the Ascendancy class who had served under various Governments, Liberal and Conservative. These officials had experience of the ups and downs of the course of politics in the country and were, to a great extent, relied upon for guidance by every Government. An Englishman, having a seat in Parliament, was always appointed as the Chief Secretary to the Lord Lieutenant. He it was who was chiefly responsible to the Government for the administration of affairs in Ireland and answered for all Irish questions in the House of Commons. The Lord Lieutenant, as representative of the King, did not take an active part in the everyday affairs of Government. He resided in the Lodge in the Phoenix Park, as did the Chief Secretary, in a separate Lodge, when not in London.

No matter how well disposed a Government may have been towards this country, the Chief Secretary was obliged to rely, to a great extent, on the information and advice given him by the permanent officials, as he had little personal knowledge of the conditions prevailing in the country. Every change and piece of legislation which was proposed for the betterment of the people was regarded with disfavour by the permanent officials of the Castle. They belonged to the minority who, in their own interest, had ruled the majority for generations and anything that threatened that rule could not be tolerated. The landlords and Freemasons all over the country had the ear of their friends in the Castle at all times and relied upon them to thwart, as far as possible, every change that tended to lift the majority out of the condition of dependence to their rule. Ascendancy, inside and outside, went hand in hand in obstructing every measure passed for the amelioration of the people's grievances. For years, the Government had troubled little about Ireland, leaving matters to a great extent in the hands of Dublin Castle.

It was only in the early 1870s that a change began to take place, under the leadership of that great statesman, William

Ewart Gladstone. He it was who first saw the need for improvement in land tenure, and secured to the tenantry, in his Act of 1870, a modicum of protection from the uncontrolled tyranny of the landlords who, up to that time, had absolute power of eviction—even though there were no arrears of rent due—without any compensation for improvements made by the tenant or his forefathers. Thenceforth a tenant, if evicted, was entitled to compensation for any such improvements. Though braking, only in a light way, landlord rapacity, this was the beginning of the end of landlordism in Ireland. Subsequently further legislation and finally Land Purchase measures enabled the tenantry, with Government assistance, to buy the landlords' titles and, in time, become absolute owners of their own farms.

Having lived for generations under this system of government, the people could see little hope of change and settled down to a condition of slavery for a mere existence. Young men, in complete ignorance of the country's history, entered the police service, unable to see that they were enlisting in a service specially organised to sustain the very system that was crushing their fathers and, indeed, the very system that obliged them to enter that service; for it was the struggle for existence in their homes that forced them to choose between emigration and joining the police. But, as already observed, it was only after a considerable time that these men began to realise how little they had known of the system of government they were employed to uphold. As time went on, more and more did they realise the nature of the service in which their lives were cast. In the early years of their service, in a position considered much better than that of young men of their class in civil life, they went on thoughtlessly, got married and settled down to continue to the end—pension time.

Here, perhaps, I should give an outline of the daily life of the men of the Force. In rural areas, as we have seen, men were scattered all over in parties of four and five. They were accommodated in ordinary houses, known as Police Stations. The towns were policed by larger parties of from ten to fifteen, according to the size of the town. There was little difference in the lives of the men in town and country. All lived under a stringent code of discipline which, if generally enforced to the letter, would have rendered life intolerable. Yet, this weapon was in the hands of the commissioned and non-commissioned officers, and much depended on the character of those men how the regulations were enforced. In both grades there were martinets without scruple, who were generally actuated by self-interest but cared little for the interests of their subordinates. To bring themselves under notice as efficient officers was their constant outlook. Previous to the agrarian struggle, discipline was not exceptionally strict, but this disturbing event brought manifold increased duties and responsibilities on the police and much more strictness in discipline.

Whether in towns or rural stations, there was a great deal of sameness in the lives of the men. If you went into one police station in a town, you could see the conditions which existed in every other police station in every town in Ireland, and the same applied to the rural stations; one rural station was a replica of all the others. The furniture was supplied by the Army Ordinance department and was similar to that in the army—deal tables and forms mounted on iron trestles, iron beds, bedding, arm racks, and arms, all of military pattern. Barrack regulations and other official matters decorated the whitewashed walls of the Day or Orderly Room; a badge and notice boards, displaying public notices outside, told the public that this was a police station. There was a morning parade of the men under arms, when they were expected to turn out clean—uniform, arms and equipment in good order. Not every morning but pretty frequently, there was practice in elementary drill and handling of arms and, after dismissal, a school in police duties. A barrack orderly was placed on duty every morning and remained on duty for twenty-four hours. He attended to calls and recorded in a diary the time of men going on and returning off duty, the nature of the duty, and all matters of importance reported at the station.

In towns, routine town duty was carried out, with patrolling of rural parts of the district as well. In rural districts, the ordinary daily duty was patrolling, together with any other duties devolving on the station. This gives little idea of the general work of the service. Every day brought something demanding special attention—investigation of crime and complaints, the collection of information and statistics, and the carrying out of instructions on all matters requiring attention. There was a roll call at 9 p.m. in winter and 10 p.m. in summer, after which men sleeping in barracks should not be absent during the night, unless on duty, and married men should remain in their lodgings. Duties of the service are more fully detailed in another chapter.

Though the life of the R.I.C. man was anything but inactive, there was a sameness in it that narrowed his outlook. It was a constant grind, studying Acts of Parliament, circular orders, *Hue and Cry*, burnishing and polishing arms and equipment, keeping barracks and premises in apple-pie order, and moving within the rigid limits of discipline. He read the daily newspapers, but little else in the shape of literature. He was part of a machine and to do the work required of him well, by those who controlled that machine, was all that was wanted of him; efficiency in this respect was as a rule more in his interest than mere literary attainment. His sources of recreation were limited. Handball, throwing weights, cycling, playing cards—though forbidden by regulation, which however was got over—small dances in private houses or in favourite public houses, practising music with violin, melodeon, and other instruments, were the chief pastimes for the single man. Married men spent most of their idle time with their families. In time one got ground into the system and did not feel its restrictions to the extent which might be expected. At all times, even during the Land War, up until 1920 there was good feeling between the rank and file and the general public, and this tended to balance other disagreeable features of the service.

Though the regulations were rigid, they were not as a rule enforced to the letter. An occasional narrow-minded officer might be found always on the lookout for small faults, and this obliged men to be on the alert for him. The men were well conducted and, in their own interest, lived within the regulations in a way that satisfied the officers in general and there was no need to be on the watch to find them committing serious violations of discipline. Head Constables and Sergeants, in constant touch with the men, saw to it that no serious irregularities were allowed to continue unchecked, and there was no need to be hunting after fiddle-faddles. Officers who did so were not at all the most useful.

CHAPTER THREE.

OFFICERS.

Officers of the Force were practically independent and safe in their position, if they only paid ordinary attention to their duties. Each District Inspector ruled his own district independently and could indulge in his own views towards the men, as he wished. He could be considerate and sympathetic or autocratic without regard for the men's welfare or feelings. Sergeants in charge of stations could be kept in hot water, by fault finding for little or no cause, which meant constant tension at the station. Some officers regarded themselves as needful for keeping the rank and file up to scratch and these were always on the look-out for something wrong. But the great majority did not go out of their way to give unnecessary trouble: there was no need to. Non-commissioned officers and men, in their own interests, were careful to live as required by the regulations. Still, an officer out for giving trouble could render the position of subordinates very irksome.

There were three grades in the rank of District Inspector and each was attained by seniority after appointment, so that they had nothing to gain by officiousness, nor was it evidence that they were the most useful type of officer; instead, they often only brought trouble on themselves. The service was so well organised that all that was needful for an officer to get along without trouble was a good knowledge of his work and a good share of common sense. Such a man gave little trouble and was appreciated by the rank and file.

County Inspectors had much more power than District Inspectors. In their hands rested chiefly promotions for, in all instances, their recommendation was necessary. They were appointed from the District Inspectorship and indeed were not always the best selection. The influence of "big houses" brought down the scales in favour of not a few of them. Some were above the average but there were others who were mere nonentities. Correspondence was their principal work but police clerks did the general routine office work. Their Inspections were mere outings for them, going from station to station every quarter and there was no one to question their movements. Their Inspections, however, were of much concern to men anxious to stand well in their estimation, if they ambitioned promotion, as most men did. The better educated, intelligent men could be observed on Inspection and, in time, usually gained the rank of Sergeant; but as shown in the chapter dealing with promotion, a sense of justice was not always the main consideration for officers in their recommendations of men for promotion. County Inspectors with two or three exceptions entered the service as cadets.

Officers generally were not of a cast iron pattern but differed widely. Some were haughtily domineering, others exacting, others petty and mean; the majority reasonable and considerate, while the whole, with few exceptions, troubled little about the men's interest, regarding them principally as needful to maintain them in their own positions. They had the cream of the service and it was for the rank and file to look out for themselves.

All cadet officers had found themselves in a position reserved for their class, affording them congenial employment, as well as a position of security and social standing. Their salaries provided a decent living and they did not need to worry; the rank and file did the worrying for them. They did not behave outwardly towards the rank and file as bigots—they dared not—but they could not be otherwise. It was bigotry that provided them with their jobs and their private lives were spent in the fellowship of bigots. ("Tell me your

company, etc.") Except in the matter of promotion, their treatment of Catholics differed nothing from that of Protestants. The
integrity of the Force as a body was outstanding and Catholics,
more than Protestants, maintained that position. Officers, therefore, could not and did not discriminate in their treatment of
men in the ordinary course of duty. On Inspections and all
other duties, all came under the same rule without distinction
and nothing occurred to show that all did not stand on the
same level. Any privileges allowed by the regulations, rewards
for services rendered or other individual matters, were treated
without regard to the religion of those concerned and the
same could be said in disciplinary matters.

District Inspectors, who had risen from the ranks, had
gone through the mill and generally were efficient officers.
They had attained the limit of their ambition and could afford
to slow down. Some had the common sense to do so, while
others thought it necessary to make everybody feel that they
were there, and code and regulations and red tape troubled
them more—far more—than was needful.

Few Catholic officers entered as cadets and they, as a rule,
got into the swim of the service, taking the line of least
resistance. There were a couple of notable exceptions, very
able and independent officers, and it is only due to their
memory that their names should find a place here. Physically
fine types, they were fearlessly just and admired by the Catholic
members of the service but detested by the Protestant members and their friends outside the service. Their superior claims
could not be denied and both became County Inspectors, after
filling important positions as District Inspectors. Their claims
to the higher staff appointments were far above officers who
had filled them; but they were not of the "Castle kidney" type
and, no more than Sir Anthony McDonnell,[1] were not wanted
there. Contemporaries—few of whom survive—who may
read these lines, will not need to be told that the officers

1   Under-Secretary to the Lord Lieutenant; see chapter 10.

referred to were I. R. B Jennings[2] and Galwey Foley.[3] Mr Foley had charge of the Crime Special Branch at the time of the Sheridan case.[4] I had the pleasure of meeting him about that time and he told me that, in the examination of Sheridan's record, one damning feature stood out, namely, that he did not charge his victims at the time of arrest—it was only afterwards that he preferred the charge, presumably when he himself had committed the crime unnoticed.

The Inspector General had always, with one exception, been a military officer of the rank of Colonel and, in the early years of the Force, his deputy and assistants had also been military officers. From the very beginning, then, the R.I.C. was organised and ruled from a military standpoint, rather than as a civil force. The amalgamation of the various county police establishments in 1836—in the words of the Act 6 Wm. IV chapter 13—"in order to provide for one uniform system of rules and regulations throughout the whole of Ireland", under one central authority, and the formation of a Depot in Dublin where recruits were trained as soldiers, places beyond question the purpose for which this Force was required and maintained without change during its existence.

Though in later years officers of the Force were appointed as deputies and assistants, Sir Andrew Reed was the only officer of the establishment who at any time held the position of Inspector General. He was the most competent of any of the Officers who filled the position, before or after him. He was a barrister-at-law, the author of a Treatise on the Licensing Laws, and a comprehensive work titled "The Irish Constable's Guide". He was an officer of broad outlook and effected many appreciative reforms in the service. The military officers had not his administrative experience as a police officer. A mind fashioned in military service could not be as fit to rule a police force, especially the R.I.C., as that of an officer who

2 Ignatius Ronayne Bray Jennings (R.I.C. 35879).
3 John Matthew Galwey Foley (R.I.C. 37562).
4 See chapter 8.

had graduated in that Force. He could not possibly have the same needful experience of all the political and conflicting elements with which the Force had to contend. The military officer could be no more than a figurehead, as compared with Sir Andrew Reed, who had served as District Inspector, County Inspector, and Divisional Commissioner, and who was familiar with conditions of life in the country from boyhood. The reforms that he effected go to show that he was actuated by liberal views in his rule of the Force. A few instances will, I think, show this.

Soon after his appointment, he issued an order that the barrack orderly, who previously had to remain fully dressed, with belt and side arms, during the night, until relieved the following morning, might, after roll call, take off his belt and side arms, unbutton his tunic, and rest on his bed placed on forms in the orderly room, but should be on the alert. Restrictions on men entering public houses for refreshment, whether on or off duty, were removed to the extent that, when not on duty, they were free to do so. Knowing the sameness of their daily lives, he ordered that men should have perfect freedom to enjoy themselves, to sing and dance and engage in any pastime not forbidden by regulations and, as far as possible, make their barracks their home. This was a departure from the unwritten law that men's noses should be always on the grindstone.

In country districts, roads were badly fenced and trespass of cattle on them was a frequent occurrence. People brought to court for road offences were fined and the cost and loss of time attending court meant much to poor people. Sir Andrew Reed ordered that before summoning people to court, they should be cautioned and only afterwards, should the offence be continued, were they to be brought to court. Other minor offences, as to names on carts, obstructions on streets, etc., were to be dealt with in a similar way. Most convincing, perhaps, of his capability as head of the Irish police was an order by him that the police should be courteous towards the public making enquiries or desiring their assistance, and directed County

Inspectors not to recommend any man for promotion who failed to carry out these instructions.

Above all other improvements that marked his rule, was the competitive system for a portion of the promotions to the various grades. In these competitions Catholics gained ninety per cent of the places assigned to each, and hence the opposition evinced by Protestants to them (as will be seen in the chapter dealing with promotion). Not only did these examinations enable Catholics to win promotion by their own ability but they demonstrated beyond question the ability of Catholics over Protestants and had the effect of compelling more liberal views of their claims in other respects.

Earl Cowper, when Lord Lieutenant [1880–2], finding Sir Andrew Reed a highly qualified administrative officer, appointed him Deputy Inspector General in 1881, and he succeeded to the Inspector Generalship in 1885, which he held with distinction until 1900. Sir Andrew Reed, it would appear, had not been giving satisfaction in Castle circles previous to his retirement. We find Mr George Wyndham, on his advent to the Castle as Chief Secretary in 1900, writing to Mr Balfour, Prime Minister, that the Police had grown rusty during years of division among the Irish Parliamentary Party *and consequent peace*, that *Sir Andrew Reed was useless*, and that with Colonel Chamberlain, then Inspector General, his deputy and Sir David Harrel, Under Secretary, "in whom he had complete confidence",[5] he had been discussing the matter and that the necessary steps were being taken to screw up gradually the efficiency of the police.

Here, we have a flood of light thrown on Castle methods and see how an Inspector General of police, under whose rule the Force had attained the peak of its efficiency, was set aside as useless. Was it because Sir Andrew Reed did not see eye to eye with the Ascendancy, inside and outside the Castle, that he was dubbed as useless by Mr Wyndham's informants?

5   The text is unclear: David Harrel was appointed in 1892 and ceased to be Under-Secretary in 1900.

Mr Wyndham had no experience of Sir Andrew Reed's services and must have relied on what he had heard of that
notably able officer who had risen, as no other R.I.C. officer
had, from the bottom to the top of the Inspectorate of the
Force. That there was more at the back of Sir Andrew Reed's
retirement from the service than came to light, could be read
in his valedictory address to the Depot Force. There was no
need for him to enter into what would seem a vindication of his
career in the service, by informing his audience that he entered
the service a friendless young man, and that on that day the
R.I.C. stood higher than at any time in its history. In that
speech, I thought I noticed a strain of bitterness and resentment.

Colonel Sir Neville F. F. Chamberlain, who had been on
the staff of Lord Roberts in Africa during the Boer War, succeeded Sir Andrew Reed. He was a gentlemanly, sympathetic
officer. He set about making some changes which he thought
would be an improvement in the service. In his efforts to carry
out his views, I heard from one in a position to know, that in
almost every point he was told that his views would not accord
with the Code. On one occasion when the Code was put up
to him as an obstacle, "oh damn the Code", he blurted out.
He served only a few years.[6]

While the officers were not unsympathetic towards the
rank and file, they troubled little for their comfort and welfare.
In this, however, it was difficult to fault them. Complaints
were not wanted and officers did not encourage the making of
them. It was only when discontent became manifest and
general that the Castle took heed.

Nothing was done to brighten the grinding life of the
service. When off duty, men could not, as in other police
forces, dress in plain clothes and feel free for the time. The
regulations were there eternally clouding their lives. Their uniform was of the coarsest shoddy and even the allowance for
making it up was not sufficient to pay the tailor, and men had
themselves to make good the balance. It was only after years

6   Not strictly correct: he served 1900–16.

of complaint that men were provided with raincoats. The accommodation for the families of Head Constables and Sergeants in charge of stations was, in many instances, scandalous. Other married men had to supplement the miserable lodging allowance of 4*s* 4*d* a month to rent ordinarily decent houses for their families.

Up to the last years of the existence of the Force, the pay and allowances of the rank and file were miserably small. On a few occasions, Commissioners were appointed to enquire into this and other grievances. On none of these occasions did the men receive any support from the officers, as it was felt that the Government was not prepared to admit the men's claims. That was always the attitude of the officers, high and low, not to encourage any movement not likely to be favoured by the Government. An instance of this attitude occurred at one of the Commissions, at which an officer giving evidence declared that a moderate increase in pay and allowances sought by the rank and file was "preposterous". This gentleman took care to be on the safe side but it is only right to say that there was hardly another officer in the service who would have so described the men's claims; and it is doubly right to add that this individual was a "ranker". Even though sympathising with the men, officers were not prepared to back them up in matters not likely to be approved of by the higher authorities.

The regulations prohibited men from assembling without authority to discuss grievances or to communicate with the Press in any way. The Press, however, was the chief means of ventilating grievances and men took the risk. The *Freeman's Journal* was read in every station and its columns were always open to the R.I.C. and, though efforts were made on the part of the authorities to get the names of men who had written letters, the *Freeman* office never disclosed them. On one occasion, a very strong agitation arose for an increase of pay, etc. In Limerick, men got rather out of hand and held meetings without permission. One of the Assistant Inspectors General hurried down from the Castle and held a kind of court martial, resulting in the dismissal, peremptorily, of five Constables. A subscription throughout the service was made up for them, every man subscribing his mite, though it was an infringement of the regulations to subscribe generally to any purpose without permission. It was carried out quietly and the authorities did not interfere. The dismissed Constables were young unmarried men and in the United States they found freedom and "made good". A Commission of Inquiry into the matter complained of followed resulting, as in other instances, in cheese-paring improvements that merely aggravated rather than allayed discontent. On another occasion, an agitation in Belfast for improvement in conditions reached a threat to strike. The authorities threatened to replace the police on the streets by military. The trouble, however, was got over by the dismissal of the leader of the threatened revolt and the transfer to counties of a number of Constables who were replaced by others from the counties.

As compared with England and Scotland, Ireland was over-policed to a very large extent and the question of cost was constantly raised in Parliament. The number of officers was far in excess of what would be required in an ordinary police force. These were good positions for the sons of needy supporters of the Government and were maintained to the full. There were few resignations of the rank and file and, at hand, an ample supply of recruits. These conditions played into the hands of the Government in dealing with any complaints as to pay and allowances. Although it could always be shown that the pay of English police was much better than that of the R.I.C., it was contended, on the other hand, that the cheaper cost of living left the Irishman as well off. An Englishman was always Chairman of Commissions of Inquiry. R.I.C. witnesses used to urge that they were not only underpaid, as compared with English police, but that the latter were not of as high a standard, educationally or otherwise, as the Irish Force. I remember on one occasion seeing the Chairman writhing in the chair with passion at such an assertion. Whatever difference of opinion there may have been on this question, it could hardly be contended but that the R.I.C. was immeasurably more useful to the English Government than any other of its police forces, and should therefore have been placed on a par with them on questions of pay and allowances.

CHAPTER FOUR.

MEN.

Needless to say that discipline for a lengthened period in any force makes its impress on the physical and mental make up of men. Being a semi-military body, this was more observable in members of the R.I.C. than, perhaps, in any other police force. Entering the service at any age, without any experience beyond the limits of their native parish, the recruitment source supplied the very material most easily fashioned as required. It was the general belief that, while their minds were in that plastic condition, Depot training aimed specially at shaping the outlook of recruits along narrow police lines. This was not at all correct. The training at the Depot was more of a military than police character; while strenuous, the training was not disagreeable. As they progressed, recruits enjoyed the drilling and life of the place, with bands and bugles reverberating over the beautiful ranges of the Phoenix Park, utilised so much for military and police training. The police band was famed for its excellence and, in summer evenings, performed on the Depot square to the delight of crowds of citizens seated around. The trained recruit on his post as sentry behaved just as a soldier, delivering up his orders to the Orderly Officer on his rounds, and in all respects carrying out his duties in accordance with military regulations. It was then he felt himself a person of some importance and not a little proud of himself. Soldiers and police, especially the Reserve Force at the Depot, fraternised in Depot and military canteens. Police sentries saluted with arms all military units passing their post, who returned the salute, and military units acted likewise towards police units. Training in police work consisted of a couple of hours at evening school until recruits had acquired a knowledge of a simple manual in catechetical form of elementary duties. On the whole, Depot training went much more to the making of a soldier than a policeman.

The R.I.C. recruit did not actually set out on his course as a policeman until allocated to fill a vacancy in some county, other than his native county. Men were not permitted to serve in their county, or in any county in which they had relations. It may have been in a city, town or rural station that he first took up duty as a policeman. He yet had no practical knowledge of police work but, in drill, was much more proficient than older men among who he took his place. He was quite confident of himself and could not understand why men having considerable service were nervous in the presence of officers, especially on Inspections. His experience at the Depot consisted chiefly of parades and inspections and the Inspector General himself would not disturb him. Years brought a change and the time came when he too perhaps found himself quite as shaky on Inspections as the old Constables of the days of his ignorance. The officers at the Depot, as in the army, behaved as gentlemen and received the unaffected respect of the rank and file, to which they were entitled. With some exceptions, so much could not be said of officers in the counties.

The future of the young policeman was entirely different to his Depot experience. Whether in city, town, or country station, it was only then his education as a policeman commenced. He took his place amongst older members conversant with the system. In cities and towns, half or more would probably be young unmarried men and in these the recruit found companionship. The country station, though not so attractive as city or town, offered other advantages in its outdoor life and, in quiet districts, humdrum, easy-going duties. No matter where the recruit found himself, he had to apply himself to becoming an efficient member of the service. Under the tuition and example of his elders, he had to set about acquiring a local knowledge of places and people, and a practical knowledge of his duties. He had as well to engage in the grind for Inspections and daily routine of the station and, in time, become more or less a qualified policeman.

The military features were, however, still maintained. It was only in the latter years of its existence that the Force was supplied with truncheons in addition to bayonets which had previously been worn on all duties and even on recreative walks. Drill was one of the subjects in which Sergeants and Head Constables had to qualify for promotion. This combination of soldier and policeman, as well as being an Imperial Force, independent of any control by the people, was, to a great extent, responsible for the dominant attitude which was characteristic of the R.I.C. They did not regard themselves as servants of the people to the same extent as other police forces, yet they did not, as was alleged, behave quite as masters of the people. Their training and discipline was of a nature that rendered them too ready to resent any interference or offence in a heated or, perhaps, unwarranted manner. They were not, however, at all inimical towards the people. They were not as a body intolerant but exercised their discretion in a generous way in carrying out their duties. They were well instructed in their duties and were able to discriminate in matters that could be overlooked or remedied by drawing attention to them. There were, it is true, members who in order to establish their efficiency were familiar figures in the witness chair in Petty Session courts but the general body were not out to harass the people by dragging them into court and causing them trouble and expense for matters which they, themselves, could as effectively settle. In rural districts, especially where they had practically a free hand in ordinary violations of the law, they gave no trouble that could be avoided and were very popular with the people. Depot training was in every way an advantage but, in time, men left it behind and in ordinary circumstances became more and more stereotyped policemen.

When acting in bodies during the land agitation regrettable conflicts occurred between the police and the people. Many of these incidents might have been avoided, if more prudence and cooler judgement had been exercised. It must be remembered that, in those days, with the ordinary law practically in suspense, and the country seething with agitation bordering on revolution, danger of conflict between police and large meetings of the people was always present and it happened that aggressive conduct towards the police was often as much responsible as want of restraint on the part of the police for many things which occurred. In bodies, the police were always acting under orders, but in some instances may have exceeded their orders to an extent not required. In baton charges, it was sometimes alleged that needless brutality took place. Occasions may have occurred when the conduct of the crowd, by stone throwing or other action, accounted for more violence by the police than otherwise might have happened. Frequently too, it happened that most damage was done by a few ill conditioned men, actuated by private or vindictive feeling, while others merely wielded their truncheons without inflicting injury. The position of the police, called upon to deal with a violent or disorderly crowd, is often very difficult and to hesitate and not deal promptly with disorder may be a mistake and only lead to further trouble. In time of trouble, in every crowd, especially in cities and towns, there are always elements up against the police, and they avail of the chance to have some of "their own back". Not infrequently then the difficulty is to apportion the blame between police and people on occasions when tempers on both sides are riled. Most blame was always, as a rule, dealt out to the police.

Some regrettable instances of firing on the people with fatal results marked the course of the Land War. The most serious of those occurred at Mitchelstown under the Balfourian regime in 1887. A large meeting of eight or ten thousand people from surrounding counties was being held in furtherance of what was known as "The Plan of Campaign". The police endeavoured to force a way through the crowd to the platform for a government reporter. The crowd resented this and a fierce conflict, with batons on one side and blackthorn sticks on the other, ensued. The police retreated to the barracks, followed by a stone-throwing portion of the crowd. Having gained the shelter of the barracks, some of the Constables fired through the windows, killing one man and fatally wounding two other men.

It can be safely said that the action of the police on that occasion was mainly responsible for that tragedy. At the time, in order to avoid trouble, permission was usually obtained from the promoters for a place on or near the platform for a Government reporter at such meetings. No such effort seems to have been made by the police at Mitchelstown but, instead, they attempted to force a passage for the reporter through thousands—many of them armed with sticks—from Cork, Tipperary and Waterford. The risk of such action should have been evident, especially at that time when the agitation throughout the country was boiling over. A prudent police officer should have seen the danger and taken every means to guard against trouble. What instructions, if any, he had on the occasion did not, of course, transpire but about that time a telegram in cipher—"Don't hesitate to shoot"—was sent by the Government to the authorities in southern counties; whether previous or subsequent to the meeting, I cannot say, but it is evidence that the Government was prepared to stand by the police in all their actions, however extreme.

Whether the people on the platform did not bear a portion of the responsibility for what happened is a question. They might say it was not their business to interfere. Even so, if it had been possible to intervene and counsel the crowd to allow passage for the reporter to the platform, the tragedy might have been avoided. After the event everyone is wiser. One thing is clear: having got to the shelter of the barracks, the police were not justified in firing. The firing may have been without orders, by a couple of men whose heads had received blackthorn damage. Only a sustained violent attack by a strong body of men, apparently with the intention of breaking into the barracks, would have justified firing.

An inquest resulted with a verdict of wilful murder against the officer in charge and some of the men, but the proceedings were quashed by the Queen's Bench on some irregularity and no further action was taken.

Another instance of firing which might have been avoided occurred in 1880 at a place called Inver some miles from Belmullet. A party of police protecting a process server was attacked with stones, as they approached the village where the processes were to be served. In the conflict and excitement, a shot was fired accidentally or through nervousness by one of the Constables. Others, thinking that an order to fire had been given, also fired. The officer in charge rushed to the front and raising his hands stopped the firing. A young girl named Ellen McDonagh received a wound from a pellet of buckshot from which she died in a few days. An inquest ended abortively, on a point of law raised by the Crown, that the coroner had not issued his precept to the police to summon a jury. Thus the matter ended. The full circumstances never came to light. The occurrence, however, was broadcast through the press as an example of R.I.C. brutality—that the unfortunate girl died of a bayonet thrust. Now the fact is there was no bayonet charge at all nor did the police get into handgrips with the people who fled when firing commenced.

There is hardly any doubt that all instances of firing might have been avoided; in fact were not justified. The Code contained the most stringent instructions on the question of firing. It was strictly enjoined that recourse to the use of firearms should be taken only in the last extremity and when all other means had failed to avoid the necessity for such a course; and men were warned that in all such occurrences, a solemn enquiry would follow and that those responsible would be called upon to justify their actions.

Once, I had personal experience of an instance where a fatal firing might have occurred, had it not been for the prudence and steadiness of the Head Constable in charge of the police. Again, it was a case of protecting a process server, at a place called Stonefield, previous to and in the

neighbourhood of where Ellen McDonagh was shot. As in
that instance, we were met by a crowd of men and women
armed with stones. Already some stones had been thrown and
some of the police hit. The Head Constable halted the party
and warned the people that, if they continued to oppose our
advance, it would be for them a serious matter. With fixed
bayonets, he ordered the police to advance. The crowd stood
their ground and stones hopped off the rifles. Again he halted
and ordered the party to load, warning the people if they did
not disperse they would be fired upon. The crowd remained
defiant and excited. The police order to "the present" was
given. The crowd was about thirty yards distant. It was not a
large crowd—not more than fifty or sixty men and women.
There were twenty police in the party, so that the people
would have had little chance if the Head Constable had persisted in forcing his way. The attitude of the crowd convinced
him that if he did, lives would be lost. He ordered the police
to lower their arms, and unload and, abandoning the attempt
to proceed further, marched the police and process server
away. He reported the whole circumstances and his action was
approved by the Castle. Eight or ten of the principals of the
riot were tried at Assizes and sentenced to from four to six
months' imprisonment. This was an instance in which the
Head Constable should have received a reward but he was an
elderly man and was satisfied when he escaped censure.

Two or three other instances of firing by individual policemen occurred with loss of life but the circumstances have
escaped my recollection.

Notwithstanding those regrettable instances of firing, it
can, I believe, be fairly stated that, in all those years of trouble,
the police did not in general carry out the many difficult
duties which were heaped upon them in an aggressive manner.
The general public were not at all affected in their daily
lives. The various Coercion Acts, giving special powers of
search to persons and houses, were not carried out in a high-
handed or [. . . text missing . . .], at all in a general manner,
due regard to the privacy of the lives of the people being

observed in instances where such searches were made. All Coercion Acts during this time were aimed at the suppression of the agrarian agitation and the police did not relish the work of enforcing them. There were no doubt individual policemen out to profit by the trouble and these did things reflecting on the general body, and were used to paint the Force in an unworthy manner. In succeeding chapters will be found full details of the difficulties with which men had to contend, and their general attitude towards the people.

CHAPTER FIVE.

DISCIPLINE.

The Royal Irish Constabulary differed from other police forces, a semi-military body drilled and trained to the use of arms on military lines, its sole purpose was not the enforcement of the civil law and the preservation of order. Even after their course of training at the Depot, the men continued throughout their service to practise drill and the use of arms. An abridged edition of the Army drill book was found at every police station and an annual target practice took place in every district. The Day or Orderly room in every station differed nothing from a squad room in a military barracks. Tables, forms of army pattern, arms ranged on racks on the walls, barrack regulations posted up, and a uniformed, side-armed orderly on duty impressed one as more like a military outpost than a police station. There was a time when the barrack orderly was obliged to remain fully dressed during the night but later was permitted to take off his belt and side arms, unbutton his tunic, and rest on his bed palliasse placed on forms, but had to be on the alert. Not only then was the R.I.C. maintained as a police force but as a military body to be employed in the suppression of any movement of a revolutionary character that might take place. Discipline, therefore, differed entirely from that of an ordinary police force.

An elaborate Code of regulations, many of them of the most stringent character, ordered the daily lives of the men. Unlike other police forces men were supposed never to be off duty. They were supposed to be available at all times. One of the rules was that if a man went for a walk, he should inform the barrack orderly before leaving where he was likely to be found if required, and report his return, which the orderly recorded in his diary. He was not supposed to go beyond a mile and a half from the barracks and not to be absent longer than two hours; even married men were supposed to come from their lodgings and report at intervals their presence to the orderly. This ridiculous rule was seldom strictly enforced. There were, however, other rules as petty and more hurtful enforced to the letter. A member of the Force was not permitted to engage in any occupation outside that of the service, even though it did not interfere with his efficiency as a policeman. For instance, he was not allowed to own a house or property in a county where stationed or, without permission, to keep a cow, goat, pig or hen—or even a dog; nor could his wife engage in, say, dressmaking, teaching or other occupations for profit. She was not allowed to keep lodgers, not even members of the service when absent from their own stations on duty. Anything likely to detract in the most remote way from the work of the service could not be engaged in by a member or his wife, without official sanction. These facts will give some idea of the daily lives of the members of the service.

The use of intoxicating drink was the great source of trouble for the men and strict rules were applied. Drunkenness was defined as "the slightest departure from sobriety". Tippling, or having the appearance of recent tippling, was regarded as an offence. Up to the 1880s, it was an offence to enter a public house whether on or off duty for the purpose of drinking; but this rule was modified to the extent that, when not on duty, men could have reasonable refreshments in such places.

The fact that such restrictions were imposed in ordinary matters will give an idea of the outlook for men if charged, say, with neglect of duty in a serious matter, or not taking proper steps in such a case, failing to carry out instructions, falsifying records, insubordination, or disrespect to a superior, overlooking and failing to report breaches of discipline, and many other possible offences. The conditions of the service

were certainly stringent but men got drilled into the system
and did not feel the pressure as much as might be expected.
Much depended on the Sergeant, Head Constable or officer
immediately responsible. Some were more independent and
considerate than others and did not go out of their way to
take advantage of their subordinates for relapses which, without much risk to themselves, could be overlooked. Others,
through timidity, or, with the object of bringing themselves
under notice as efficient officers, were less considerate. On the
whole, except in occasional instances, much fault could not be
found with the way in which such a high standard of discipline
enjoined by the regulations was carried out. In overlooking
serious violations of the rules, there was always risk that some
ill-disposed member, if reported for an offence, would bring a
back-charge against the officer reporting him, of having overlooked other offenders. There was a deterring rule in such an
event that, if a member bringing a back-charge failed to prove
it, he himself was liable to punishment, and not the other.
Charges should be made at the time of occurrence not at a
later date—hence the rule.

The punishments were very severe for serious violations of
the regulations. For minor offences, reprimands or admonitions
were doled out but, for serious breaches, severe punishment
resulted. Fines, ranging from £3 to £5, would be inflicted and
often a transfer at a man's own expense to another station. If
serious breaches were repeated within a short time and a
final warning had no effect, dismissal from the service was the
end. It was drink almost in every instance that led to a man's
dismissal. Some men could drink galore, without coming
under notice, while others would become noticeable after a
few drinks. These were the men that generally fell and their
only hope was to avoid drinking altogether.

It was not, however, the punishment at the time that
affected men so much as their record of the offence. All
punishments were recorded in the official register and these
records told against a man's advancement; not only that, but
up to the late seventies, a deduction was made in a man's

pension on account of unfavourable records so that, say, for an offence of simple drunkenness he was punished throughout life. This extremely harsh punishment was eventually abandoned. Later still, it was provided that, after a blameless period of five years, unfavourable records ceased to tell against a man in any way. This excessively harsh system of punishment was modified only after many years of enforcement, which will give some idea of the treatment men received before the advance of education began to penetrate the crustaceous establishment of the Irish police.

The disrating of Sergeants and Head Constables for disciplinary offences was a severe form of punishment for, once reduced to a lower grade, there was little hope of ever again regaining former rank, so keen was the competition for promotion. This punishment affected a man all his life for it meant a reduction in pay and pension. The reduction of a Head Constable seldom occurred, as he was always at headquarters, where responsibility was shared by an Inspector and a Sergeant. Sergeants in charge of rural stations were less secure, as each was directly responsible for control of his station. Laxity in maintaining his position often led to a Sergeant's downfall, as he could not safely enforce discipline if not himself independent. Here and there, were always ill-conditioned men who if charged themselves might retaliate by complaining that the Sergeant had overlooked offences by others and, perhaps, similar offences to that brought against him. There was no disrating of Inspectors. They might be severely reprimanded if the complaint was not serious, but, if of a serious nature, they would be called upon to retire from the service.

Every facility was given to a man charged with an offence to defend himself. Charges were made in writing and the man called upon to admit or deny the charge. If he admitted the charge, he could forward any statement he wished in mitigation of the offence, or appeal for leniency. If the charge was serious and denied, a Court of Inquiry consisting of two officers was appointed. The court was on the lines of a court martial in the army. Every chance was given to the accused to defend himself. A copy of the charges and the names of the officers who were to constitute the court were supplied to the accused before the date fixed for the assembly of the court, which was open to the public. The accused might object to any of the officers appointed but this right was never availed of. The accused was permitted to employ legal aid for his defence but this assistance was more restricted than in civil courts. The witnesses were sworn and their evidence taken down in writing. The entire proceedings, with the finding of the court, as well as any statement the accused might wish to make were forwarded to the Inspector General who confirmed in whole, or partially, but seldom fully disagreed with the finding of the court and he it was who measured the punishment, if any. These courts were regarded as quite impartial.

With the many pitfalls to be avoided, inside and outside the service, men felt the pressure of responsibility and the need to be ever on the watch. That was the atmosphere in which they lived their lives. It was only when they discarded the uniform, went on a holiday and the pressure removed that they realised how heavy it had been. Their hearts became light, they felt different men and enjoyed themselves to the full.

This chapter is intended to show how discipline was enforced and must be taken with other chapters to get the full conception of the difficulties that bore daily on the lives of the men of this service.

CHAPTER SIX.

INSPECTIONS.

Though the Code of regulations was very stringent, it was not the difficulty of conforming with the regulations, as much as the constant grind to which men were subject, that rendered service in the Force irksome. There was a monthly Inspection by District Inspectors and a quarterly inspection by the County Inspector, as well as periodical inspection by Headquarters superior officers. On these Inspections men were expected to be found proficient in drill, having a good knowledge of the police duties and all matters making for the efficient discharge of their duty. County Inspectors were responsible for the efficiency of their county, District Inspectors for their district, and Head Constables and Sergeants for their stations. Men were, therefore, being constantly schooled and had to study Acts of Parliament, circulars from Headquarters on all sorts of matters, commit to memory descriptions of offenders in the *Hue and Cry*, as well as to be able to show a good practical knowledge in all circumstances bearing on the detection of crime. Inspections by County Inspectors and District Inspectors were made without previous notice, so that men had always to be prepared for them. Some of those officers were narrow-minded, an occasional one intolerant—their chief concern often on Inspections being to find fault. At one time a County Inspector could on Inspection impose a fine up to 10/- there and then upon men for some fault on parade. This authority was withdrawn to the extent that, before inflicting a fine, he should return to his station and consider the matter, with any explanation the alleged defaulter may have made in writing. This course put a stop to fines on Inspections, as the papers in due course were forwarded to Headquarters, and probably would suggest that the matter did not call for such punishment, being due for the moment, perhaps, to the mood of an intolerant mind. While County and District Inspectors were practically secure in their jobs, all, nevertheless, kept in view inspections by high officers, and the need to stand well with the Castle.

The result of these Inspections was recorded in a book kept at each station. If the Inspection was favourable, all concerned felt relieved, for it meant relaxation of the daily grind at least for a while; but if otherwise, then the fault, whatever it may have been had to be remedied if possible; if possible, I say, for the fault may have been the outcome of a petty mind or tyrannical disposition. These officers regarded themselves as highly important individuals and were accustomed to a condition of absolute servility by the rank and file. If men wished to stand well in their view, they should always be careful to assume an attitude of profound respect in their presence, standing at attention and punctuating their conversation by "Sir" without limit. The outlook for men in the service was to a great extent in the hands of the officers. Not only were the officers in a position to be helpful to their subordinates but sometime or other might be in a position to injure them and this was always present to the minds of men in adopting a ready attitude of respect and obedience.

At a moment's notice, a County or District Inspector might enter a station and order the men to parade for Inspection. If all the party was not present, the absentees should be accounted for. On parade the men were minutely scrutinised. They should be clean shaved, with hair cut short, uniform, arms and appointments clean and well fitting. Leather parts should be polished to shine, and brass and steel parts glittering, arms free from rust and serviceable, and all in accordance with regulations, including the shoes, which should be of the high-low, or what was known as the "derby" pattern, without toe-caps. If the party present was large enough, drill and rifle exercise was gone through. After "dismissal" a thorough inspection of the barracks followed. Every room was entered and expected to be clean and in order, especially the dormitories, in which the bedding should be clean and neatly folded on the bedsteads in military fashion. The bedding consisted of a straw mattress and bolster with a supply of blankets and top covering. A feather pillow was not allowed. Some officers were small enough to examine the folded mattress to see if it contained one but most officers took no notice if the pillow was concealed from view.

Each man had a box of regulation pattern which contained a kit outfit. This kit consisted of a suit of plain clothes, a pair of shoes, shirt, socks, towel, shaving necessaries, knife, fork and spoon, square of soap, and blackening; all supposed to be needful in the event of men being ordered to a distance from their station on duty likely to be of some duration. In fact, this kit was never taken into such use; it remained in the box during the entire service of its owner and kept clean and in order for Inspections alone. Yet this box and kit were minutely inspected on every occasion. Its conception seemed to have been something in the nature of a wartime emergency, when men might be called up to proceed to a centre of trouble. This box and kit were one of the greatest sources of trouble. Contrary to what might be expected of police officers, many of them were not without fads. The box was painted black outside and red inside. Tape was attached to the inside of the lid by brass tacks and divided in sections, in which razor, knife, fork and spoon, and other articles fitted. One officer might expect the paint to be vermilion and the tape of a particular pattern and colour, another might order the red to be a common dull shade and an entirely different class of tape, and men had to carry out the change as required. Even the arrangement of the kit in the box was not always the way every officer required. Though this box and kit were a source of hot water to men throughout their service yet, strange to say, the box was one of the things many of them retained after retiring on pension, as a memento of their servitude; only one man did I know to be an exception. One day, as he looked at the box and recalled all the heartburnings it had brought him, he removed it to an outhouse and, taking up a sledgehammer, smashed it into matchwood!

The Inspection of the barrack completed, an examination in police duties followed. This consisted of a test of knowledge of Acts of Parliament and practical police work. Recent legislation, if bearing on political or agrarian trouble, always received special attention. Coercion Acts were drafted so as to take in every form of action to be regarded as an offence. There was a lot, therefore, of "watching and besetting", "using intimidation to or towards any person or persons, with a view to causing such person or persons to do an act which he or they had a legal right to abstain from doing"; "or abstain from doing an act, which he or they had a legal right to do, or causing to be done", etc. etc. All these tongue twisting complexities had to be got off verbatim, and that required some practice. Men did not bother much about the *Hue and Cry*, as the descriptions were generally guess work and of little value, except in the case of physical defects or marks, and there was usually some hasty coaching of one another when getting ready for the parade, as to colour of eyes and shape of noses, etc. Lynch was never a stumbling block. His description could be reeled off pat. It will be remembered that he escaped from police escort and eventually from Maryboro' prison, where he was undergoing penal servitude.[1] The Inspection finished; men were dismissed. Then the books and records of the station were examined and the result recorded in the Inspection Book.

At every station there was, of course, a crimes register in which was recorded all prosecutions by the police of the station. Some officers used to refer to that record to see the number of prosecutions each man had to his credit. This, however, was not a general practice by officers. It was rather an objectionable thing to do, as a good policeman was not to

---

1 Presumably refers to some notorious case.

be judged by the number of petty cases he had at Petty Sessions and besides it looked as an incentive to men to be over-officious. The class of officer who had recourse to such means was not actuated for the public good but rather by the desire to see the public harassed by the police. Not all the officers it must be said were unreasonable and came to give trouble. By many, their Inspections were a mere formality and their visits were not a source of uneasiness. These officers were popular in the service. There was no need for so frequent Inspections, as the Force had after years of discipline and schooling been brought to a high standard of efficiency, and half the Inspections could have been dispensed with, which would have been a relief to everybody.

CHAPTER SEVEN.

PROMOTION.

Promotion was chiefly in the hands of the County and District Inspectors, especially County Inspectors. It was on the recommendation of County Inspectors that promotions were made by the Inspector General. County Inspectors were not obliged to follow the recommendations of District Inspectors though no doubt they were influenced by them. Men recommended had, of course, to come up to the standard of qualifications required but there was no regular system. Officers held different views of the fitness of men for promotion and these views were not always free from bias of one sort or another; it might have been religion, not sufficiently active in the discharge of duty, not acquitting himself on Inspections to the satisfaction of the officer, or other cause which should not have been applied in a matter affecting seriously the position of a man in the service. While some of these officers rightly considered that the claims of senior men, other qualifications being equal, were entitled to priority, others took a different view and ignored seniority on the ground that the men were too old, although in other counties much older men were being promoted. Thus, while men of eight or ten years' service were promoted in some counties, in other counties they would not be promoted until they had served twenty years or more.

County Inspectors were frequently changed from one county to another and then the system of promotion was liable to undergo a complete change in these counties. In one county a man might have been on the top of the promotion list when the change took place. The new Inspector came along and said this man was too old and struck his name off the list and thus the man was deprived of the promotion he should have got and probably never got beyond the rank of Constable. At the whim, if not a more reprehensible view, of an officer, this man was injured during his life, not only in his salary while serving but in his pension. Many of these officers had no sense of justice in their recommendations of men for promotion; it was not with them a question of balancing carefully as it should have been the merits of men in order to be fair and just to them. Promotion lists were confidential documents and men had no knowledge of the changes which were made in those lists or the grounds, if any, for making them and had no means of redress by appeal or otherwise. Occasionally, on Inspections by Headquarters' Officers, men did complain of being passed over and, in the absence of any valid reason, were as a result of their complaints promoted. It required some courage on the part of a Constable to make such a complaint for, of course, it raised the question of partiality or want of care on the part of the officer concerned.

The foregoing applies only to the promotion of Constables to the rank of Sergeant in the ordinary or general way. To attain a higher rank than Sergeant it was as a rule necessary to get the first promotion early in one's service, as seniority in the rank of Sergeant had much to do with promotion to the rank of Head Constable and later to that of District Inspector. If a man did not get promotion to the rank of Sergeant before he had twenty years' service, he had little chance of further advancement. This is how men often suffered by the irregularity of the system.

About 1888, Sir Andrew Reed, Inspector General, introduced a system by which 60 appointments to the rank of Sergeant were given every year to Constables of five years' service and upwards who had gained the first sixty places at a competitive examination in literary subjects conducted by the Civil Service Commissioners. This was a great incentive to young Constables to study and improve their literary knowledge. Sir Andrew Reed presented a gold watch every year to the Constable who obtained first place at the examination. Men who passed this examination were known as "P" men and were not required to undergo any further literary test for any higher rank. This took the promotion of the successful candidates entirely out of the hands of the officers and they were strongly opposed to it. They held that these men spent their time studying subjects that interfered with their efficiency as policemen. This was not at all true. Instead, these men were much more efficient policemen than their fellows of inferior education. Complete subservience to their control was what the officers required and anything that rendered men independent of them was not wanted. These sixty Constables gained promotion every year by their own efforts independently of officers' views and besides it was seen that Catholics were gaining almost all the promotions under the system. Protestants relied more on religion and Freemasonry than on literary merit, while Catholics seized the chance of winning promotion by honourable means, which they might not hope for in ordinary circumstances. Opposition to the system was continued in an underhand way and carried into higher circles, with the result that the number of annual appointments was reduced to thirty. The sixty appointments were only about one quarter of the promotions of Constables every year under the ordinary system, of which, as we have seen, there was no regular method. In that system there was a qualifying examination not beyond the capability of most Constables but qualifying at that examination did not mean eventual promotion, as vacancies for all were not likely to occur. These promotions were entirely in the hands of the officers.

Promotions to the rank of Head Constable up to around 1888 were made chiefly on the recommendation by County Inspectors of Senior Sergeants, and Sergeants although not senior who had a good record of what was known as "good police duties". A qualifying pass in literary and police subjects was necessary. Then there was a small proportion of Sergeants who had been successful at the competitive examination in literary and police subjects promoted to this rank. Sergeants who had served six years as chief clerks in County Inspectors' offices were also promoted to the rank of Head Constable.

Up to the 1880s, promotions of Head Constables to District Inspectorship were sparsely made and these were chiefly Protestants. By degrees, these promotions were increased until half the vacancies were filled by the appointment of Head Constables, the other half by the Cadet system. Head Constables were promoted from two lists—the seniority list, and of men, although not senior, who had passed the "P" examination and afterwards were successful at a competitive examination in professional subjects—law, police duties, and drill. It was open to Sergeants and Head Constables to undergo the "P" examination and, if successful, they were not subjected to any further test in literary subjects for any higher rank. "P" indicated passed and they were known as "P" men. The test approached but was not quite as difficult as that for admission to the Customs Service at the time. Sir Andrew Reed stated that it was equivalent to the qualifying test for admission of cadets at the time he entered the service. Head Constables and Sergeants, who had passed this examination, were then eligible regardless of seniority to compete in professional subjects for a specified number of places as vacancies arose in the rank of District Inspector and Head Constable, respectively. The idea was to give intelligent ambitious men an opportunity of improving their literary and professional knowledge and gaining promotion without having to wait for the slow and uncertain seniority method.

This system had one serious defect. Everyone was satisfied that the Civil Service part of the examination was quite an impartial test. Here, the candidates were known to the examiners only by numbers; not so at the examination in professional subjects, where the candidates appeared in person before the examining board of officers. This part of the examination was certainly open to favouritism. Where only a few marks might mean the success or failure of a candidate to get one of the places assigned to the competition, he could be easily placed there. The value of answers of questions in Acts of Parliament and police duties was entirely in the hands of the examining board. Some of the candidates may have been previously known to, or may have served under, one or more of the officers constituting the board and, in appraising the value of the answers, which might not differ very much in merit, it was easy to award a few marks one way or another. Unquestionably, then, this part of the competitive examination for Sergeants and Head Constables had not the confidence of the competitors, especially in the case of Head Constables competing for District Inspectorship. These promotions were seldom made on merit alone. The Inspector General himself had not always a free hand in these appointments. From time to time, it was manifest that merit was not the prevailing consideration in the promotion of Head Constables, whether by seniority or competition.

Dublin Castle might have been rightly placed as a Freemason and Orange Lodge combined. It is needless then to stress the value of having at one's service fellow Freemasons and Orangemen, especially if they manned the outposts of the Castle itself. Officers in many instances were members of Masonic and Unionist clubs in every district. The Protestant members of the rank and file were in close association with members of those clubs, if not members themselves. In these clubs, the merits and demerits of the local police came under review from time to time; for these people had the presumption to assume that their views of the administration of the law should be taken into account. In a country where religious and political feeling entered so much into the lives of the people as in Ireland, officers frequenting those Protestant political clubs could not avoid being influenced in their recommendations of men for promotion. Instead of it being regarded as highly objectionable, it was rather a matter for approval for officers or men to be members of such clubs.

Another feature in connection with these competitive examinations was that the examination papers were printed in

Dublin and were in the hands of Castle officials before the examinations took place. Policemen were employed in the Castle as clerks and orderlies. It was not an impossibility then for some of the candidates to have seen the papers previous to the examination. The lengths to which men were prepared to go to gain promotion can be measured by the fact that on one occasion, at least, a Sergeant got a civilian to personate him in uniform at the literary part of the examination conducted by the Civil Service Commissioners. During the examination the fraud was discovered and, of course, the Sergeant was dismissed the service.

The entire system of promotion—so varied and admitting of so much unfair selection, in a service where special care should have been taken to be just, as far as possible—was the cause of much sourness and resentment. Religion unquestionably was always in the background of promotions, the only exceptions being the young Constables whose success was confined to literary subjects by the Civil Service Commissioners.

Up to 1875, there was scarcely a Catholic Head Constable in the service. Only by degrees, as the standard of men entering the service improved in education and otherwise, rendering such discrimination too glaring, was the rank of Head Constable opened to an appreciable extent to Catholics; and only about the year 1888, after years of complaint through the Press, were half the vacancies in the rank of District Inspector given to Head Constables. Even then, Catholics did not get a fair proportion of the appointments in the higher rank, to which their numbers in the service entitled them. From time to time, circulars were issued by the Inspector General warning men that having recourse to the use of influence would not only be regarded as highly improper but would raise the question as to their fitness at all for promotion. This was proof that outsiders were constantly urging the claims of individuals on the authorities. There were, notwithstanding those circular warnings, people who could with impunity and without any risk of hurt to those they wished to serve walk into the Castle and have carried into effect the promotion of any man, if at all eligible. Catholics received a greater percentage of promotion to the rank of Sergeant than to that of Head Constable or District Inspector because of the number of stations, consisting of small parties, all over the country in charge of Sergeants. To the rank of District Inspector, Protestants received about half the appointments. Some of those promoted from the seniority list would not qualify for the rank of Sergeant, if obliged to rely on their own ability.

In Dublin there were zealous old ladies associated with proselytising institutions and religious meeting places. Members of the R.I.C. found their way there and constantly attended those religious functions—wives of Castle officials also attended. A notable feature in connection with those institutions was that the R.I.C. patrons were, in the course of time, promoted one after another, some to the rank of District Inspector.

Again, when Head Constables, without any outstanding qualifications, were raised to the rank of District Inspector over the heads of others much more competent, it was found that those men had been stationed in the environments of castles that housed the descendants of those who had stood by England, when Ireland was fighting for her existence, and were still pillars of Dublin Castle; or, it might have been their luck to have been stationed in a place where a Chief Secretary and ladies of his entourage had been accommodated on his tour of the Gaeltacht; or perhaps had distinguished themselves in the Smith Barry, Clanricards, or other centre of trouble, during the Land War.

Whether he willed it or not, the Inspector General was obliged to accede to powerful political members of the Ascendancy, for whose upkeep the R.I.C. were there.

Once, on the occasion of an Inspection by the Inspector General, of a county Headquarters station at which I was present, he made a special note in his Inspection minute of the excellent answering in police duties of a young Constable of seven years' service. Now this Constable was only of mediocre intelligence and in no way superior or equal to other

Constables present. Soon after, his promotion to the rank of Acting Sergeant came down from the Castle. It was necessary to justify the promotion of this man over the heads of other Constables of fifteen or twenty years' service on the parade and hence the special reference to him in the Inspection minute. The Inspector General, no doubt, had got his orders from a source that could not be denied. Inquiry led to the discovery that this Constable, before entering the service, had been in the employment of a notoriously active Unionist political leader.

Under the authority of a Catholic officer or non-commissioned officer, Protestants never felt happy and often had recourse to the cowardly method of thwarting if possible the promotion of Catholic Head Constables to District Inspectorship, by anonymous letters to the Castle. Of this I had personal knowledge in three instances. With regard to two Head Constables, it was alleged that they had national sympathies rendering them unfitted for Inspectorship; in the other, on account of the number of his children, he would be unable to maintain the dignity essential to his rank. Outsiders knew little of and were not concerned by the prevalence of writing anonymous letters with regard to promotions in the service. The Head Constable with the family obstacle got a friend to lodge to his credit a sum of money in the bank, to which he was able to refer. To the chagrin of the bigots, he was promoted in due course and filled the position with credit. Of the two alleged nationalists, one might thank the Orangemen of Belfast for his promotion. Shortly before his turn for promotion, another Head Constable during riots in Belfast had been chaired on the shoulders of Orangemen in the streets of the city. To pass over the nationalist and promote the Orangemen's darling could not be done, so both received the commission. The other Head Constable though highly qualified was not so lucky and, with other equally qualified men, got no further. The lucky one was the man referred to elsewhere who was not afraid to display his underclothing and pride in the fact that it was of Irish manufacture. Yet at the same time he was a strict disciplinarian, living himself strictly within the regulations and requiring all under him to do the same.

Religious preferment up to 1880 was unabashed but the agrarian trouble during the next twenty-five years, with Sir Andrew Reed's enlightened rule of the Force, brought a much more liberal treatment of Catholics in this respect. Even still, bigotry was there. About the middle of the 1880s this incident occurred—in county Headquarters, the Head Constable referred to above[1] paraded the men of the station and informed them that it had been represented that Catholics in the service were not being fairly treated in the matter of promotion and that he had been directed to ascertain their views of the allegation. It was a most unusual occurrence to put the question openly to the men in this way. It was probably calculated that the answer would be a flat denial of the statement. Catholics had to be careful of their attitude on the question. The question was put straight to them and it was a chance not to be missed. There was silence and hesitation in the ranks until a Sergeant spoke and said that in his view Catholics were not fairly treated in the matter of promotion. All Catholics on the parade as well as the Head Constable concurred; Protestant members remained silent. The nature of the communication that led to this incident did not transpire but if more such incidents had occurred it would have been all to the good.

In time of trouble, when the Force was badly needed, *religion did not matter so much.* During the rebellion of 1920, when the Castle was inundated with resignations, religion went by the board and Catholics were promoted wholesale to all the grades including Inspectorship, and pay and pensions were more than doubled.

1   It is not clear to whom Fennell refers.

CHAPTER EIGHT.

FAVOURABLE RECORDS.

What were known as "Favourable Records" were awarded with frequent money grants to men who had shown what was regarded as exceptional ability in the detection and conviction of offenders, and for acts of bravery. These records were classed 1st, 2nd, and 3rd. First and third class records were awarded for good work in bringing to justice criminals; second class for spirited conduct in preventing possible loss of life or injury to the public such as, at great personal risk, stopping a runaway horse, rescuing a person from a burning building, or such other act. Second and third class records were of little value more than approbation but first class records helped men very considerably on the road to promotion. To gain these records was, therefore, a great incentive in the pursuit and conviction of offenders. These records contributed not only to early promotion to a higher rank but told thereafter in further promotion. Up to the Land War, first class records were awarded only in serious criminal cases such as murder, robbery, burglary. During that struggle, these rewards were held out to men active in the enforcement of the various Coercion Acts, and in obtaining convictions for agrarian offences. By the creation of new offences a wide field was open for police activity and unscrupulous men were out to make the most of the opportunities that offered. Success in obtaining convictions for agrarian offences took first place in the award of first class records and money grants and, in some instances, special promotion. Serious offences without agrarian features were relegated to secondary consideration in the matter of reward. In agrarian matters, men felt that their action would not be too closely sifted and they were not always particular in dealing with offenders or suspected offenders.

In two or three instances, non-commissioned officers actually committed or were privy to the commission of crime in the hope thereby of gaining promotion. In one instance a Head Constable named Whelehan [R.I.C. 29264], in County Clare, employed a police spy named Cullinan to organise a raid on the house of a farmer who had become unpopular. The Head Constable with a party of armed police were in ambush when the raiding party, among them the spy, arrived. In the struggle to arrest the raiders, the Head Constable was killed [on 11 September 1887] and others of the police injured. Three or four of the raiders and the spy were secured, while some escaped. A nolle prosequi was entered against the spy who was produced as a witness at the trial of the others. They were sentenced to four or five years' penal servitude but were liberated after a short period.

In another instance, a Sergeant named Sheridan [R.I.C. no.?] committed the crimes himself, and in one instance had a man imprisoned for eighteen months for the commission of one of these crimes. Mutilating cattle was a very reprehensible class of crime, often committed during the Land War. On patrol one night with a young Constable in a country district in County Leitrim, they met a young man named McGoohan at a late hour coming from a dance. He was quite a harmless country boy. Sheridan arrested him and brought him to the barracks. He then with the young Constable returned to where they met McGoohan. He told the Constable to keep watch on the road until he had a look around a nearby farmyard. After some time, he returned to the Constable with the tails of two cattle, stating that he had found them in the cow house cut from two of the cattle. He returned to the barracks and charged McGoohan with the crime. Next, he returned alone to the farmyard, bringing with him McGoohan's boots with which he made impressions in the soft ground about, and afterwards took plaster casts of these impressions to prove that McGoohan had been there. McGoohan was tried at Assizes at Sligo, convicted and sentenced to eighteen months in gaol, which he served. The young Constable supported Sheridan at the trial but was shaky in his evidence. The barrack orderly's evidence, detailing what occurred in the barracks, especially the fact that it was only after he returned the second time that he charged McGoohan was not helpful. But those were the days of jury packing, when men were convicted on evidence strained against them to the limit. Sheridan was awarded a first class record and a money grant in the case.

He next represented that on account of his activity in the locality he was not safe from attack and asked for a change to another county. Active men were always posted to disturbed districts and Sheridan was transferred to one of those in County Galway. He was not long there until he had a boy convicted of setting fire to a rick of hay. It did not transpire whether it was himself fired the hay but in all probability it was, for he had not abandoned his methods of getting to the front.

But Nemesis awaited him down the road—if not around the corner. Young inexperienced Constables were not likely to stand up against the act of a Sergeant, and Sheridan always selected such a man to accompany him when he had in view the concoction of a criminal charge. In the instance which proved to be his downfall, he had previously posted up one or two notices warning all and sundry to have nothing to do with an evicted farm in the locality. This was a common method of intimidating people not to rent or touch in any way an evicted farm to the prejudice of the evicted tenant. With a young Constable, Sheridan then set out to look for a victim, bringing with him a few copies of the notice he had posted up. They entered a public house to have a drink and there met a man who appeared to be a tramp; when the man left they followed him. Sheridan arrested him and searched him slipping at the same time into his pocket copies of the notice he himself had brought with him. He conveyed the prisoner before a

Resident Magistrate and charged him with posting up the notice. The prisoner requested a private interview with the Magistrate and satisfied him that he was a police officer on detective duty in the district and that the charge was faked. The Magistrate discharged the prisoner. An inquiry resulted in Sheridan's dismissal from the service. Instead of arresting him and placing him on trial for the crime, the Government gave him time to escape and, when the warrant was issued for his arrest, he was gone. The Irish Party charged the Government in the House of Commons with conniving in Sheridan's escape and raised a storm of protest over this, and the Whelehan case. Public opinion in England became tensely aroused, and Sheridan's trial would have been a damaging exposure of Irish administration; and so he was allowed to escape.

About this time, McGoohan was discharged from gaol and immediately went before a Magistrate and made a declaration that he was innocent of the crime for which he had suffered. Sheridan's record was examined by a very independent officer who at the time was in charge of the Crime Special Branch [i.e. J. M. G. Foley]. A very convincing feature appeared as a result namely, that in every instance in which Sheridan had been rewarded, he first arrested his man but did not charge him with any specific offence at the time. It was only afterwards when he himself doubtless had committed the crime that he charged his prisoner. There was now no doubt about McGoohan's innocence, and what was termed a "compassionate grant" of £200 was given him by the Government: a paltry sum for the terrible injustice done to him.

In another instance, a Sergeant named Sullivan [(R.I.C. . . .] was charged and put on trial for writing an anonymous letter of an incriminatory character in an agrarian matter in the Mallaranny district, but the jury disagreed and no further proceedings were taken. No other instance of malfeasance came to light but there was a good deal of suspicion that in some instances it was represented that things happened that did not occur.

Kerry was one of the most disturbed counties during the Land War. On more than one occasion ambushing parties reported that they had encountered raiding parties who had fled after an exchange of shots, but no one was hurt or made amenable. Although nothing serious happened, the idea would have been to gain credit and reward. No hurt was inflicted on anyone beyond intensifying the dragooning of the people and saddling them with the cost of extra police. For each county there was a fixed free quota of police; while for extra police in consequence of disturbed conditions, the county had to pay half the cost. A high-handed Resident Magistrate named Clifford Lloyd was posted there but his arbitrary methods brought about his recall as a result of the Irish Party's action in the House of Commons. General Buller, after his return from the Boer War, was sent to Kerry and during his time conditions improved considerably. He remained there for only a short time.

Some executions took place the justice of which was doubted by many. Myles Joyce, who was executed for being one of a party who murdered a family in a place called Maamtrasna, County Galway,[1] declared his innocence on the scaffold; also a young man named Hynes, in Galway, and another named Barrett, in Kerry, of whose guilt there were grave doubts. In the existing turmoil and confusion of the times, when strict supervision of the police was difficult if not impossible, things may have been done by individual members which would not bear scrutiny in the light but nothing in the shape of organised illegalities could occur. The R.I.C. as a body were the most upright police force in the world and, no matter how ill disposed an individual might have been, he would have difficulty in finding an accomplice.

Sheridan, who was eventually brought to book by officers of the Force, selected inexperienced young men in the country stations to accompany him carrying out his plans and, having

1 This incident is described in Jarleth Waldron, *Maamtrasna, the Murders and the Mystery*, 4th edn (Dublin: Edmund Burke, 1993).

led them a certain distance, they found themselves enmeshed and unable to see their way out of the difficulty. Neither would the authorities, though encouraging activity, approve of questionable methods in obtaining convictions. A feature of the standing orders was that nothing in favour of an accused person should be withheld but given in evidence as well as that against him. It is worthy of note that the Constable who accompanied Sheridan in the McGoohan case was called upon to resign. The Constable in the other case resigned voluntarily and was granted a small gratuity, as he was not guilty of any offence.

It cannot, of course, be gainsaid that the incentive to obtain convictions was there, and there were individual members of the Force who would risk the commission of criminal acts to gain promotion. A half yearly return of rewards for good police duties showed that the principal rewards were for work in connection with the agrarian trouble. Thus were the police urged to be active in the aid of landlords, by holding up to them the rewards that awaited them for this work and it was this knowledge that led some men to think they were safe in adopting methods, however extreme and shady, in cases where landlords' interests were involved.

The Clanricarde, Smith Barry, De Freyne, Lugacurran, and other outstanding centres of trouble were the favourable hunting ground for "Favourable Records", as was evidenced by promotion of men employed there to the rank of Head Constable and eventually, in some instances, to the rank of District Inspector. Nothing like the Whelahan and Sheridan methods would at all be countenanced nor would the Force have it for, though subservient to their rulers in carrying out their legal duties, they were the very class of men who would boldly stand up against anything in the shape of malpractices in the service.

CHAPTER NINE.

CORRESPONDENCE.

In no other police force, perhaps, was there so much correspondence and red tape as in the R.I.C. Correspondence entered into the daily lives of officers, Head Constables and Sergeants in charge of stations, and no duty required more attention or caused more worry. County Inspectors had a chief, and one or two assistant clerks. Previous to the Land War, the Head Constable assisted the District Inspector but during the agrarian trouble a clerk to each District Inspector was appointed, and Head Constables relieved, to enable them to give more time to outdoor duties.

Foolscap was employed. Each half sheet was divided lengthwise by a crease into two equal halves, the left half being used for the original statement, the right being reserved for the observations of superior officers. Rules governing the method, from the crossing of the *t*s, to the dotting of the *i*s, had to be explicitly followed. Reports embraced every conceivable matter with which the Government had to be kept informed. If something appearing in the daily Press, of which the Castle should have been made aware and that a report had not reached it before it appeared in the Press, attention was drawn to the matter and a statement of facts called for. A man known as "Scissors and Paste" was specially employed to read the Press and bring to official notice such publications. If of any importance, and a report had not been made, the officer responsible would have to explain his remissness and guard against a recurrence of it.

Reports and returns were required periodically: some weekly, some monthly, and others half yearly. Omission to render any one of them on the date fixed brought the defaulter a reminder by next post calling for it, with an explanation of the neglect. A list of reports and returns, with dates on which to be furnished, was posted up in every office and, if trouble was to be avoided, that list should be consulted every morning. Returns differed from reports, as the former were generally of a statistical nature and were supplied on tabulated forms in manuscript. Serious crimes—indictable offences—had to be reported on special forms having printed headings containing specific questions, such as time and place of offence, date and hour when reported to the police, date and hour when scene was visited by the District Inspector, etc., thus summarising the facts, and making it clear whether police action was prompt; a detailed report then followed. Evictions were also reported on similar forms, giving the names of the landlord and tenant, number of police employed, whether a case of hardship, etc.

Previous to 1879, office work was very light but the Land War brought a big change. Officers as a rule relied more on their punctuality and efficiency in correspondence to establish their worth than on most of their other duties. They had daily opportunities in this respect of bringing themselves under notice. For every class of information the Government relied on the R.I.C. and, during the Land War, county and district offices were engaged without limit of time. Reports and returns were being called for daily, on all sorts of matters and conditions in every county. Parliament when sitting made constant demands on the time of the Force. The Irish Parliamentary Party was a disciplined solid body of over eighty members led by Parnell; it was always in opposition, resisting the passage of Coercion Acts, raising questions and debates on the action of the police, and the administration in general. Reports and statistics were constantly required by the Chief Secretary to enable him to answer questions and complaints brought before the House.

The R.I.C. officers, reading the press reports of these debates, learned the attitude of the Government on the questions raised and were always able to play into the hands of the Chief Secretary. So too, reading between the lines, they could interpret Castle despatches for required information. For instance, if it was desired to show the country in a bad state, say, of boycotting, intimidation, or such offences that could not be checked by the ordinary law, returns would include cases that should not appear at all as such. Again, when it was wanted to show an improvement, as a result of coercion, there would be a considerable reduction in the criminal statistics. These returns could not be checked. Seldom if ever were the thousands of questions bearing on the condition of Ireland truly answered in the House of Commons. Dublin Castle framed the answers and the Chief Secretary stood by them. The answers were usually a blank denial, a justification, or a sidestepping of the facts. The police officers always took care in their reports not to give expression to views likely to run counter to the Castle.

With its network of organisation and training, the R.I.C. was a ready source of information of life in the country and was availed of by every Government to the fullest extent. Correspondence was the greatest source of worry in the service, especially to Sergeants in charge of stations, and was made the medium by narrow minded officers to give unnecessary trouble. A simple subject might attain a file of several sheets with passages marked "A", "B", "C", and perhaps other letters of the alphabet, requiring further elucidation, or drawing attention to some non-observance of sections of the Code. Unfortunate Sergeants in charge of stations became immaturely grey from heckling and worry and longed for the day when they would shed the uniform and send the Code and all that it meant to the devil! It was only part of the system which fashioned the R.I.C. as a most effective machine for governing a country against its will, as Mr. John Morley[1] once observed.

1 John Morley served as Chief Secretary twice: in 1886 and 1892–5.

Mr. Morley's other reference to the R.I.C. as "eyes and ears" of the Government has often been quoted as evidence that espionage was one of the most useful services rendered by that Force. There was nothing further from the truth and Mr. Morley did not intend any such interpretation of his words. As Chief Secretary for Ireland in Mr. Gladstone's administration of 1880, Mr. Morley found the R.I.C a most efficient service in supplying information on the many questions and complaints raised frequently in the House of Commons by the Irish Parliamentary Party. No espionage was needed for this service nor for many other similar services. They were merely matters of public note of which the R.I.C. had daily experience and, as already shown, was a ready reliable medium of supplying that information. This work devolved chiefly on District Inspectors and Sergeants in charge of stations. It did not concern the rank and file who above all were not spies. While living and moving constantly among the people, the R.I.C. drew the line of officialdom and avoided undue familiarity which is not the attitude of spies. Their military training inoculated them with too much of the soldier to be even good detectives and they prided in their status as being above the ordinary policeman.

There was a detective branch of few men—not more perhaps than twelve or fifteen—who moved about in civilian dress as tradesmen or other occupation and took employment in different places. These men might be regarded as spies. They were not known even by the local police. In one instance, one of them employed as a blacksmith in a small town used to get drunk, or feign it, and get arrested by the local police. Only afterwards, when action had been taken against the chief political leader of the place and the blacksmith had cleared off, did it become known that he was a detective.

Another instance was that of the detective who circumvented Sergeant Sheridan in his criminal deeds. He had been known in the locality as "tramp Ryan". After that event, "tramp Ryan" disappeared and, though guessing took place, it was not with certainty that his identity was ever known, even by members of the ordinary police who regarded these detectives and the Crime Special Branch, referred to in chapter 8, as more likely to bring trouble upon them than help.

That the R.I.C. as a body was a force of spies is one of the most groundless allegations ever conceived; as groundless as other allegations that they were pampered and patted on the back by the Government when, in fact, they were harassed carrying out hateful duties, without the least consideration—without the least recompense—beyond their stinted pay and allowances. In the troubled years of the Land War, the action of the police was frequently questioned in the House of Commons by the Irish Party. The Government as a matter of course always defended and praised the police. This is about the amount of patting they received and the R.I.C. were able to appraise it at its proper value: instead of being an incentive, men did only what they were compelled to do and Dublin Castle saw to it that there was no shirking of the work. Instead of engaging in espionage, men's minds became soured and resentful and they did nothing they could safely avoid doing, naturally of course.

CHAPTER TEN.

BIGOTRY.

Throughout its history, care was taken to officer the R.I.C. almost exclusively by Protestants, while the great majority of the rank and file were Catholics. While the officers were of the ruling minority, the men were of the subject majority. A gulf separated the two classes. It was always asserted by its rulers that this Force was outstanding in its detachment from religion and politics, as every police force should be, in the fulfilment of its purposes, but it cannot be supposed that such conditions were characteristic of a Force specially organised and trained to sustain one class say, twenty-five per cent of the people, whose interests conflicted violently with those of the other seventy-five per cent; nor were they.

Let us glance at the oath administered to recruits on their entry into the service [see chapter 1]. Here are the concluding terms of it: "that I do not now belong, and that I will not, while I shall hold the said office, join, subscribe, or belong to any political society, whatsoever, or any secret society, whatsoever, unless the society of Freemasons". It cannot be denied that Freemasonry, above all others, is an oathbound society, the violation of whose secrets entails the most dire consequences; and that part of their sworn obligations is "to prefer a brother in all their dealings and to recommend him to others as much as lies in their power". Nor can it be questioned that Freemasonry has been the constant enemy of Irish aspirations, and the Catholic religion. Yet this was the only secret society that members of the R.I.C. were free to join and Protestants as a rule availed of the privilege. Once, a member of another police service wrote to an experienced friend in the same service for advice as to the best means to gain promotion. A copy of the letter and the reply chanced to come into my hands. The reply of the old experienced friend was to the effect that political influence, if sufficiently powerful, was good but that Freemasonry was best. Not only in the R.I.C. but also in every other service of the Government this agency was found at work.

I may here state that, in the discharge of their duties, the oath at entry never troubled the men of the R.I.C. It had been to them a matter of course, of which they had little conception at the time. The writer can say for himself that when he entered the service he did not know what a Freemason was. I can imagine some reader ejaculating "where the devil was he reared". Nevertheless it is true and, I have no doubt, in many other instances as well.

It is true the regulations applied equally to all ranks and set up a high standard of rectitude to be observed. Notwithstanding, bigotry and prejudice were live factors in the background. If there was no other evidence the assertive attitude of Protestant members in the ranks was sufficient to show that they were not in doubt as to their position in the service—that theirs was a position of confident security as compared with that of Catholics. Not only that, but their general attitude in the discharge of their duties and otherwise was that the regulations should not apply to them with the same strictness as to Catholics members. They were never at home under a Catholic officer. Their attitude was something analogous to that of their co-religionists outside the service—that they were of the superior or privileged class. This was chiefly observable in district and county headquarters, where they were usually in larger numbers than in rural stations. As far as they could safely go, the Protestant members were highly partisan but the law and regulations were there and they had to conform to both, though not infrequently in a manner indicating how they felt at being ordered about by Catholic superiors and, if Catholic officers or non-commissioned officers asserted their authority without discrimination, it was given out by Protestant members to their friends that such officers were bigoted towards them and, by circulating lies and writing anonymous letters, tried to injure them in the service. Inspectors were independent and could ignore such cowardly action, so might most Head Constables, but the malicious intent was there and was generally aimed at the most upright, independent non-commissioned officers, especially Head Constables on the way to promotion.

Bigotry in the service was constantly in evidence not alone in the matter of promotion but in the behaviour and speech of Protestant members in the ranks. They were not afraid to give expression to their feelings on political matters and the stronger the opposition they evinced towards every National movement the better they thought was their chance of advancement, while Catholics had always to be carefully on their guard to say little or nothing, unless they were of the flunkey type—and there were a few of them around everywhere—who always joined with the Protestants in their views of everything having a political or anti-national tinge. Flunkeyism was one of the means adopted to gain favour in official circles by men having little else as a recommendation, who availed of every opportunity to show how worthy they were as loyal and reliable members. The better educated and more independent Catholics avoided discussion of subjects on which they were supposed not to have any views. Religious matters were never discussed but politics was so much bound up with religion that political matters could not be discussed without religion standing out in the background revealing the mind of the speaker. As an example, at the time Archbishop Croke took the lead in the revival of Gaelic Athletic Sports, I heard Protestant policemen speak of the Gaelic Association as a "murder gang", and Land Leaguers would be referred to as "highway men".

Protestant shops were patronised by Protestants in preference to Catholic shops—if only to buy a newspaper they would travel a distance to leave the penny in a Protestant house. Outside Ulster, they could not very well discriminate in the discharge of their duties between Catholics and Protestants. In Ulster discrimination was always evident. Protestant demonstrations and meetings were tolerated to a much greater extent than those of Catholics. Protestant officers and men were at heart as Orange as members of that Association. Catholic policemen were afraid to discharge their duties independently and fairly between the religious sections, while Protestant members had no such caution to exercise. The matter of religion was always present. When a strange policeman arrived at a station, the first question that came to the minds of the community was "what was his religion".

Generally, the Ascendancy were always intermeddling in matters concerning the police. If anything happened of which they did not approve or in any way affected them and of which the police had not taken notice, it was a cause of complaint and received official attention. Their attitude was that the police were there specially to look after them and no one else; and, in the face of long experience, they were justified in taking that view. In some Protestant pocket communities, they would require that a Protestant Sergeant would have charge of the police station if one were there, and the request was usually acceded to. Police stations were established convenient to the residences of landlords and other magnates who as a rule were Protestant, and the men were required to pay special attention to them and their property and, not only that, but those people expected the police to be accommodating in connection with their private household affairs. Special attention was required to the roads along which they travelled and, if any wandering cattle happened to be there, the police responsible for the district were brought to account. Some of those may have been people having such influence with official sources that the police felt it prudent to be as obliging as possible. In fact all over the country, the police knew that, while they might not trouble about the ordinary community, it was well to avoid running counter to the views of those having influence with the ruling authorities. In the matter of public duty it could not, however, be said that the police were influenced in the discharge of that duty nor was it expected by the authorities that they should be; still, that feeling of the need to be careful was always present and to be in a position to meet any complaint which might be made by those people.

Again, all the public offices from the Castle down to the Petty Sessions courts were, with few exceptions, manned by Protestants, so that there was no escaping the fact that the country was run by the Ascendancy in the interests of Protestantism. The police, largely Catholic, was ruled by Protestants and there was no getting away from the need on the part of Catholic members to be doubly careful in their speech and action. While the regulations throughout inculcated upright, fearless action in the discharge of duties, these regulations were never impressed on the men in the perpetual schooling in law and detection of offences. Violations of the law included new offences created by various Coercion Acts. Crime in the country consisted chiefly of political and agrarian offences and convictions for these offences were the one concern of the authorities, while remissness or what possibly might be regarded as such, meant trouble for the police. Here, again, religion stood out; for on one side was the Protestant Ascendancy to be sustained and, on the other, the Catholic population to be suppressed.

A Liberal Government was supposed to be more friendly to Ireland than a Conservative Government. It was always noticeable that when a Liberal Government was displaced by a Conservative one, officers became more strict and arrogant, but when a Liberal Government came into power, it had a chastening effect upon them. Under a Liberal regime, the police had not such a free hand and complaints regarding their action received more attention. Gladstone, the great Liberal leader, realised that coercion was no remedy for Ireland's trouble; while Lord Salisbury's was manitobia and twenty years' of firm government—in other words, twenty years of coercion and free emigration for the discontented to the wilds of manitobia. On the occasion of Gladstone bringing forward his Home Rule measure of 1886, there was no screening of the attitude of the Protestant officers and men of the Force. Some officers, on their Inspections, spoke in a way that plainly suggested that the men should revolt against the passage of the Bill.

Sir Anthony McDonnell, who had been a notable success as an administrator in India, was appointed Under Secretary to the Lord Lieutenant in 1902[1] at a time when even a Conservative Government, under the premiership of Mr A. J. Balfour, the one time uncompromising coercionist, began to adopt a more generous attitude towards this country. Sir Anthony was a Catholic and was known to have sympathetic and liberal views, although not in favour of full independence for Ireland. Much, however, was expected from him but, notwithstanding his admitted ability and experience, he found it impossible to effect any change in Castle methods. Officials of the various departments and leaders of the Ascendancy throughout the country joined hands in thwarting his efforts to improve the administration of Castle rule, which had become fixed, with little variation—whether the Government was Liberal or Conservative—for generations. Leaders of the Ascendancy, who hitherto had free access to the Chief Secretary's office, found Sir Anthony not so accommodating as was his wont. Stipendiary Magistrates visiting Dublin had been in the habit of paying a call. Sir Anthony used to meet them at his office door and tell them that they were lucky to have so much spare time on their hands and wished that he could have the same leisure. Officialdom and Ascendancy throughout the country joined in sneering amusement at Sir Anthony's presumption in attempting to improve Castle methods. I heard R.I.C. officers refer jokingly to him as the "Bengal Tiger" but that his growls did not trouble them. Sir Anthony himself declared that throughout

---

1   Should be 1900; he served until 1908.

his career he never experienced such intolerant bigotry as he did while in Dublin Castle.

Every change of Government could be seen in the attitude of the Protestant officers and men as clearly as among their co-religionists throughout the country; a Liberal Administration foreshadowed possible changes they did not want, while Conservative rule meant leaving things as they were, if not worse.

To rule Ireland, from 1870 onwards, cost the English Government from twelve to fourteen million pounds annually. Now a great, if not greater, portion of that money found its way into the pockets of the Ascendancy. With few exceptions, all Government departments from the Castle down to the lowest office were manned by Protestants of one sort or another. These officials spent their incomes among their own party. They mixed exclusively with Protestants in clubs, entertainments and pastimes. They patronised Protestant hotels in preference of those of Catholics. For all their needs, they went to Protestant shops. The people receiving this preferential patronage employed or patronised other Protestants and so on down to the lowest grade. Thus, the money employed to govern the country and for which the general public were taxed flowed through the arteries of the Ascendancy, nourishing and sustaining it. Here is an instance: of the many returns furnished by District Inspectors of the police one, at the beginning of every year, was on hotels in his locality. This return was for the information of public officials and showed the hotels in the order of fitness. If one owned by a Protestant was there and could at all be recommended it was placed first. District Inspectors knew that the atmosphere of a Catholic hotel was not appreciated and if possible did not show it as best. In the course of their work through the country, officials found at the Castle the list telling them where to lodge. The horse and car was the chief means of locomotion through the country and, if one was needed and could not be supplied by the hotel, that of a Protestant, if within reach, was employed. The only public money which Catholics got a share of was that spent by Catholic members of the R.I.C. They did not discriminate but went wherever they got the best value.

As in the public service, the same conditions were found in the mansions and estates of landlords. Agents, stewards, gamekeepers, gate keepers and all the higher posts were filled by Protestants; Catholics did the menial work. The banks were staffed chiefly by Protestants. On the railways, too, the principal appointments were held by Protestants, and similar conditions were found in all public institutions.

Thus, the entire system of Government and life in the country was altogether in the interest of the ruling class. Centuries of misrule had placed them here, and there was no question of their right. The people had become inured to their position and toiled year in and year out without hope of change, regarding it as their lot. The general body of Englishmen could not understand why the Irish people were never content under English rule. They were always told that we had the same laws as they had and that there was no reason why we should not be satisfied. But they did not know how different were the conditions and how the law was administered in Ireland as compared with England, else, I believe, they would not have tolerated for long such an unjust, tyrannical rule in their name. The ordinary Englishman is a fair-minded, honest man, according to his lights; but political leaders and a venal Press had always kept him in darkness regarding the government of Ireland.

The only hope of the Ascendancy to maintain its position unimpaired was to keep the English people in ignorance of the rule that was being perpetuated on the Irish people and so, when it was seen that a change of view was taking place in England, their leader, Carson—then Sir Edward—started a movement known as "The Carrion Crow Campaign". He enlisted in this disreputable service some of his fellow barristers and influential magnates and he and they stumped England, not confining themselves to misrepresentation, but lying, in depicting the Irish people in a degenerate and hopeless state of depravity. One of the mercenaries outstepped all limits of decency, telling his audiences that "over there" the people had reached such a condition of barbarism that they buried their dead in sacks.

Those are the people who ruled Ireland for generations, stopping at nothing to maintain their position. Bigotry and hatred of the people, and everything Irish, were their chief characteristics. Educated in their schools and imbibing their prejudices from boyhood, the majority of the Officers of the R.I.C. could not escape a similar mentality. But in an intelligent and highly disciplined Force, as was the R.I.C., whose Catholicism was staunch and fearless, officers had to be careful to avoid any outward action that might be set down to religious feeling. It was in the ranks, as already instanced, that one found less restraint.

CHAPTER ELEVEN.

THE ADMINISTRATION OF THE LAW.

English laws are supposed to be the fairest in the world. Much, however, depends on how the law is administered. For Englishmen in England, the law in recent times has been justly administered; but for Irishmen, even in England, the same could not always be said, especially when the cause was of a political character. In Ireland, it can be safely stated that the law has not been fairly administered. Until very recently, the law has been administered for hundreds of years by a small minority, differing in race, religion and outlook, holding nothing in common with the great majority of the people. Placed in position here and given over the lands and natural resources of the country, of which the people had been robbed, this minority sustained by British bayonets ruled and dispensed the law in the interests of themselves and their class. What was to the advantage of the majority was opposed to that of the minority and, down through the centuries, the conflict between rulers and ruled lived, the majority rebelling, the minority, with English aid, repressing. So that the majority might be reduced to complete subjection, they were denied education for generations while the minority had placed within their reach the means of acquiring an education which enabled them to govern as they willed. Even when afforded a modicum of education, the majority had been reduced to such a condition of ignorance and poverty that their children received only a very elementary knowledge, fitting them for no higher position than that occupied by their fathers—hewers of wood and drawers of water. To read and write a letter when they went to America or elsewhere was all they needed and any more was a waste of time—that was the educational outlook of most people for their children.

Coming down to the period covered by this book, we see the system of Government still in the hands of the minority. Dublin Castle, the seat of Government, is manned by the minority and down through the entire system, from the High to the Petty Sessions Court, the same conditions are found. The judges, law officers, crown clerks, stipendiary magistrates, lieutenants of counties, sheriffs, sub-sheriffs and, up to the early 1890s, ordinary justices of the peace, the principal officers of police—the entire system was in the hands of the Ascendancy party. Educated as their masters, this minority regarded the majority not only as inferior but in every way as of little account, except for paying rent and taxes. They asserted their position with arrogance, exacting on the part of the majority an attitude of slavish recognition which, up to the Land War it must be said, was rendered them; and any show of independence was a thing which should be kept in check. Could it then be expected that the Government in the hands of such a party with England at its back would dispense the law justly between man and man, with such conflicting interests always in the background?

Previous to the grant of Local Government and the establishment of County Councils in 1900, the power to levy taxes for county purposes was vested in the Grand Jury. This body consisted of landlords and county squires, whose property valuation reached a certain standard. They were summoned as required to attend the Assizes of their county. They were regarded as the custodians of law and order and were addressed as such by the presiding judge on the condition of the county. Portion of their work in the first instance was to examine witnesses on oath, with reference to bills passed to them by the Crown, of cases returned for trial at the Assizes and, if satisfied that the evidence was sufficient to warrant trial by a Petty Jury, they endorsed the bill accordingly and returned it to the judge; if not so satisfied, they rejected the bill which was said to be "thrown out". Having dealt with all the bills, the Grand Jury proceeded to deal with fiscal matters, such as road contracts, the condition of the roads, county cess, claims for malicious injury to property, and other matters.

Now, those gentlemen were to a man of the Ascendancy class. They had power to assess and collect taxes for county purposes and awarded damages for malicious injury to property. This was a law existing only in Ireland. It was imposed by the British Government to safeguard the property of the Ascendancy. The object of this law was that when injury to this class was committed and when the people did nothing to assist in the vindication of the law they should pay for the damage; in other words, when they did not become informers, they should be made to suffer—something equivalent to requiring the people to become wardens of Ascendancy property.

Now this law left room for a good deal of looseness in its administration and claims were often granted under questionable circumstances. It was common knowledge that in awarding compensation Grand Juries were not as exacting in awarding claims made by Protestants and political adherents as in those made by Catholics. There is generally a motive for the commission of crime and this was one of the chief features deserving consideration in those cases and, when no other motive could be assigned, religion or politics served its purpose and the claim was granted with little hesitation. A common class of claim was the burning of hay, and injury to cattle. Injury frequently occurred where the presumption was stronger that it was the owner himself, rather than another, who set fire to hay which had become damaged by heating or other cause and of little value. Old cows and horses found dead in dykes and other places into which they had probably stumbled or perhaps the carcase deposited, after death from natural causes, were not infrequently urged as malicious acts and compensation awarded the owners, in absence of evidence to the contrary. While the police and people could oppose claims coming before the Grand Jury, sufficient evidence was not always forthcoming and, in such circumstances, compensation was often awarded, however strong the suspicion of the *bona fides* of the case might have been. Compensation in such cases was raised by taxing the people of the county, or an area of the county if the circumstances showed that the act was likely to have been committed by someone within that area. Bias on the part of Grand Juries was evident all over the country.

Thus the people were taxed by an irresponsible body independent of the people and this was one of the most glaring features of misgovernment in Ireland—taxation imposed by a body on which the people had no voice.

When at last a measure of Local Government giving the people a modicum of power in local affairs was granted, there was an outcry on the part of the Ascendancy that such authority should not be placed in the hands of a disloyal, ignorant people and for long they hoped that the Government would relent and repeal the measure. When the County Councils began to function, a policeman by order of the Castle was placed on duty in the Council Chamber, ostensibly to be useful to the Council, but the real object was for him to note and report confidentially anything in the proceedings which might reflect on the Council. This went on for a couple of years, until the espionage seemed unlikely to yield the wished-for result. The County Councils took over from the Grand Juries all fiscal affairs.

In every county the Grand Juries were the backbone of the Ascendancy and posed at every Assize Court as the chief authority in the county. The Judge's address to them at the opening of criminal business of the court justified the view they held of their position as, in addition to a reference and instruction regarding the bills to go before them, he would refer to the condition of the county, as shown by the police report made to him. If the county was peaceable he congratulated them; but if in a disturbed or restless condition, he dwelt upon the matter sometimes in severe terms, urging strong measures in the interests of "law and order". Many of these addresses were severely criticised by the National Press as political harangues and altogether out of place in his capacity as judge on the Bench.

This was the position of the Grand Juries, without anything to recommend them beyond the valuation of their members' property. They might have been able to lay claim to education above the average but this was employed only to enable them more arrogantly to do the work allotted them. That arrogance was specially displayed as they strutted around at Assizes time as the people of account. There was no auditing of the Grand Juries' accounts except by themselves and probably many of the walls enclosing their parks and demesnes were built at the expense of the people, on the plea that it was necessary to protect their property from public trespass.

Let us now see how the law was administered in trial by juries of criminal charges. In ordinary cases, free from religious or political features, no exception could be taken to the method of trial. But where charges were mixed up with religion in one form or another it generally influenced the result. This was seen in trials having a party complexion. Such cases were confined to Northern counties. In trials at Petty Sessions, such as assaults or trouble arising out of processions, the local magistrates who were chiefly Protestant crowded the bench, and judgement as a rule favoured the Orange side. Even in trials by jury, Catholics in such instances had not much hope of justice; there was no need for jury packing there. Outside Northern Ireland, religion did not affect the course of justice in any of the courts. An objectionable feature, more general in Southern than in Northern counties, was the canvassing of magistrates, previous to trials at Petty Sessions, to influence the finding of the court. This would be generally in matters of little importance to the public, such as breaches of the licensing laws, cases in which a certain result might seriously affect the position of an individual, apart from the decision of the court. Though objectionable, no injury came to anyone and, if the magistrates were influenced in such cases, the course of justice did not suffer to any degree.

In cases, however, of a political or agrarian nature there was a wide difference in the procedure outside Northern counties. From the initial stages, nothing was left undone to obtain convictions. The evidence was assiduously collected and arranged, link by link, so as to leave no loophole for escape. The Assize Courts were notable for what was known as jury packing. One Crown prosecutor for his efficiency in this respect earned himself an unenviable sobriquet, which will go down with his name in history, if it be ever recorded there.

Here is how a jury was packed: the jury list was arranged by the sub-sheriff and he summoned as many as he considered sufficient for the Assizes. The list was carefully gone through in the Crown Solicitor's office, assisted by one or two policemen who had a knowledge of the religion and politics of the jurors summoned. The names of those who could not be relied upon to convict were marked. This marked list was before the Crown Solicitor when the jury was being empanelled and when the names of the unreliable jurors were called out they were ordered to "stand by". The prisoner had the right to "challenge" I think twenty without cause and as many after as he could show cause for challenge. The Crown had the right to order any number to stand aside without showing cause and thus had the overriding advantage in having a jury composed of men likely to return the verdict sought.

The Assizes was held every six months for each county. A winter Assizes was also held in provincial centres during the Land War and cases from various convenient counties were tried at each. The winter Assizes was established in order to bring to trial without undue delay persons in gaol awaiting trial. An Assizes was regarded as an important event and was conducted with elaborate detail. In addition to men engaged as witnesses, a large force of police was brought from other stations of the county to assist the local police in preserving order in the court and streets of the town. There was little need for this, beyond adding prestige to the event. On their arrival at the railway station, the judges were met by the High Sheriff of the county with a splendidly appointed carriage and pair—the motor was then only in its embryo stages—and as the judges stepped from the train they were saluted with arms by the police guard of honour under the command of an officer. As the carriage sped to the court house four mounted police (or soldiers if stationed there)—two in front and two behind—with drawn sabres formed an escort, policemen posted at various points saw to it that there was no obstruction in the way of the cavalcade; the whole, proclaiming to the public who stood aside the Majesty of the Law! Arrived at the court house, the judges accompanied by the Sheriff, his liveried bearer of the white rod leading, passed between two lines of police who were called to attention in stentorian tones by an officer. Soon after, the judges entered from their rooms—one the Criminal, the other the Civil Court. Chief interest was centred in the Criminal Court and when the judge entered in robes of scarlet an atmosphere of tense attention was created; the Court crier's call for silence was quite unnecessary. The members of the Bar and all who had been seated stood up, the judge bowed and took his seat. The Grand Jury had already occupied seats near the Bench and the Clerk of the Crown, having administered the oath to them, the judge addressed them as already described and instructed them on the bills to go before them for consideration. The preliminary stages gone through, the Grand Jury retired to consider the bills and little delay occurred until a "True Bill" enabled the Court to proceed with the first trial.

Inside and outside the Court policemen maintained order and saw that the passages were kept clear for the movement of members of the Bar and their attendants in and out of court. Assizes was a time when officialdom became very important and the police were expected to be at their beck and call whenever they were about.

Some County Inspectors availed of the occasion to draft to the town a much larger force than was needed. It gave them an opportunity not only of adding to the importance of the event but of impressing the men with their own magnitude by minute inspection and drill parades. On occasions I saw men ordered to parade in "Marching Order", a wholly unnecessary and ridiculous order. "Marching Order" meant parading with full kit in a valise strapped on the back, as if proceeding to the scene of rioting where they were likely to be housed in a body, in what was known as a "straw lodge"—a spacious building with straw to sleep upon. The chance of getting a large body of men together did not often occur, and the inspecting and drilling and finding fault was likely to impress the men with his power over them. It must be said that all County Inspectors were not of this class and did not go in for torturing men, but there was such an occasional one.

In the town or vicinity, the judges were accommodated in some gentleman's residence during their stay. An armed sentry was posted outside day and night being relieved at intervals. There was little or no need for this as a precaution but it told the public that Her Majesty's judges were inside.

During the entire period, the police on duty were under strict supervision and every man felt the need of attention to the duty assigned him. When the business was finished and the judges sent on their way, with the same ceremonial display as on their arrival, the police gave a sigh of relief and sought needful refreshment.

It is well that our courts and judges should be respected by the people and this respect is given to them now that the people have got control of those institutions, without staging a form of intimidation as in the past.

The lower courts, held quarterly for every county, were presided over by a County Court Judge, who held the appointment for one or two counties. Both civil and criminal business were triable at these courts but limited by degree, the more important and serious cases going to the higher courts. Under the Local Government Act, all claims for malicious injuries, previously dealt with by the Grand Jury, were tried by the County Court Judge. Criminal cases tried at these Courts, being less serious than those tried at Assizes, recourse to jury packing was not so evident; yet whenever possible, barristers and solicitors often tried to wedge in matters, though not in evidence or relevant, connecting the opposite side with Land League features, in the hope of prejudicing the Court against the other party. This was more noticeable in the lower courts, and went to show that judges and magistrates were considered by members of the Bar to be prejudicial towards Land Leaguers to an extent that would influence their judgements. For thirty years, the Courts were employed with all sorts of land troubles, and Land Leaguers were regarded as a sort of outlaw by those who ran the Courts, especially the lower courts. In one County Court of which I had some personal experience, the barristers and solicitors on occasions would try, by hook or by crook, to get in something connecting the opposite party with League movements and if they succeeded the result of the trial was generally foreshadowed.

Up to the 1890s, the ordinary justices of the peace, south as well as north, were chiefly Protestants. John Morley, as Chief Secretary, set about modifying the scandal to some extent by the appointment of Catholics in every district. Such an audacious innovation in the administration of the law raised a storm of protest in Ascendancy ranks. The idea of Catholics sitting in Petty Sessions to have a voice in dispensing the law, even in minor offences, was something not easily understood. Except for appearance sake, these appointments had no effect on the course of justice; Protestants still remained the majority. It is an example of the mendacious mentality of the Ascendancy at the time. Some of the "big bugs" refused to sit with such "scruff" and never afterwards adorned the Bench with their presence—yet the Bench got on without them.

In the same period, additional police were drafted from southern counties to assist in quelling riots in Belfast. While there, they were obliged to fire on Orange rioters who kept sniping at them from side streets and covered positions. Three or four Orangemen were shot and others wounded. The city authorities and prominent Orange leaders called on the Government to have the extra police withdrawn and that, with the local police, they would establish order. The extra police were withdrawn and when the trouble settled down the city authorities told the Government that strange police should not again be sent to Belfast, but that the city police should be increased, so as to be able to deal with any outbreak in future. Never afterwards were police from southern counties drafted into Belfast for duty. They were referred to as the "Fenian Police" and "Morley's Murderers". What a contrast with the "Don't hesitate to shoot" telegram, sent to the police authorities about the time of the Mitchelstown tragedy! [See chapter 4.]

This discrimination in the enforcement of the law in northern counties as compared with the rest of Ireland was not confined to isolated instances; it had always been so. Orange processions in Ulster were, and still are, a constant source of turbulence and cost in the suppression of riots, and compensation for damage to property. One of the ablest judges, Chief Baron Palles, at the opening of an Assizes in Belfast, in expounding the law in cases of riots to come before him stated that, under the Party Processions Act and the Common Law, the Government had ample power to put a stop to those processions but the Government took no heed; their statesmen instead were aiders and abettors of those illegal assemblies.

To behave in a manner likely to lead to a breach of the peace renders a person liable to be required to enter into recognisances to be of good behaviour and, failing to do so, may be committed to gaol for a period. Apart from 12th July celebrations, Orange drumming parties frequently went about in town and country in the most provocative fashion, sometimes halting opposite Catholic houses, the drummers dancing in circles, something after the fashion of a Negro war dance. Instead of preventing such conduct or summoning the leaders to give security to be of good behaviour, the police were usually there to see that they were not molested. In other parts of Ireland, it was and is a common method of dealing with persons behaving in such a way likely to lead to a breach of the peace to require them to give security not to do so, or else serve a period in gaol. If the law had been enforced impartially, North and South, drumming parties would not have masqueraded with impunity, leading periodically to assaults and riots. Catholic excursion parties travelling through Protestant districts, even by rail, were liable to be attacked by stone throwing parties, the stones crashing through the carriage windows, often wounding the excursionists before they had time to get below the windows. Even children going a distance in small bodies to religious ceremonies had to be protected by police patrols on the roads along which they travelled. This spirit of intolerance, fostered by British Rule, has been wholly and entirely the root and branch of Protestant bigotry, not only in Ulster but in every part of Ireland.

If party processions were banned and the law administered impartially, that spirit of intolerance existing in Northern counties for generations would soon disappear and all classes would become better neighbours and get away from the narrow, miserable views, so characteristic of that part of Ireland. But this has not been the desire of British statesmen who from time to time visited Belfast and from public platforms counselled the Orangemen to "keep their powder dry" and that "Ulster would fight and Ulster would be right" should any attempt be made to curtail the privileges they enjoyed.

Later, we have Mr Lloyd George's action and the Feetham Commission [Boundary Commission] to make sure that the Protestant Ascendancy should rule, if not in the whole, at least in six counties of Ulster.

CHAPTER TWELVE.

THE LAND WAR.

The Land War changed entirely the position of the police. The short-lived revolts of 1848 and 1867 left conditions in the country even worse, and the people continued to live as best they could; there seemed no other outlook before them. Year in and year out they slaved to keep a roof over their heads and, if able to do so, were content. If evictions took place previous to the 1880s, they did not bring the police into conflict with the people. Those evictions were taken as a matter of course and the police were not required to interfere notably at them. The sheriff and his bailiffs were able to carry them out without trouble, so helpless had the people become and only a few police were usually present. The duties of the police, therefore, up to 1879 were not exacting, consisting of ordinary duties in towns and villages, and patrolling in rural districts. On the whole, men had quite an easy time. They mixed freely with the people, joining in their social functions which indeed were limited and simple at the time—athletic sports, regattas, race meetings, small local dances were the principal events. They were not called upon and did not go out of their way to give trouble. Life in the service was not at all unpleasant. An increase of pay in 1874 brought forward a better class of recruits and, in the general conditions of the time, there was no objection to young men entering the service. They did not realise that they were enlisting in a service specially organised to sustain a system which had crushed their people for generations and which was the very cause that impelled them in their ignorance to engage in that service; nor was it at all at once that they did discover it. It was only as the struggle against the system continued and their duties were multiplied tenfold, that their education developed. The enforcement of the various Coercion Acts, the protection of landlords and their agents, of "emergency men", land grabbers, and all the other duties in connection with evictions and boycotting became the chief work of the Force for years, everything else being a secondary consideration.

The landlords were the backbone of the Ascendancy and war upon them meant war upon the entire garrison. Although the Protestant farmers, north and south, had no objection to sharing the benefits of each gain by the movement, they took no part in the struggle. On the contrary, they stood aloof from it. The dethronement of landlordism meant the weakening of British rule in the country, which had so long been the sheet anchor of Protestantism in Ireland. On one side was ranged the Catholic population and on the other the landlords, Freemasonry, Orangemen, and all the camp followers of the Ascendancy with the Government at their back. It was then, and then only, that the R.I.C. had their eyes opened. They found themselves the chief instruments employed to keep in subjection their kith and kin in the interests of the enemies of the faith and freedom of their country. The greater number of them had gone so far that there was no turning back. Married men with families, without any special training or qualification—the idea of resigning their job and facing the world in search of another could not be considered.

Gladstone's halting Land Act of 1870, intending to stay the hand of the evictor, had little effect. Landlords had still power to increase rents and, during the next decade, there was no diminution of rackrenting. During that period the Irish peasantry were reduced to a condition of servility and helplessness difficult to equal. Over the entire country, the big house cast its shadow of oppression, the tenantry humbly acknowledging their servitude towards it; not only to the master did they bend in slavish humility, but even the hirelings of the

Establishment prudence told them it was well to have as friends.

As time went on, landlords became more and more repressive. Extravagant living led to mortgaging of estates. Many of the landlords, failing to find sufficient pleasure on their estate, lived a good deal in England and on the Continent. Rents were increased to meet the increasing cost of dissipation until, at last, the people could no longer bear the burden. The time had come when an effort was needed to stay the hand of oppression and, in 1879, Michael Davitt, at Straide, County Mayo, standing on the ruins of the home of his childhood, from which his family had been evicted, called upon the people to band themselves together to overthrow the system which had inflicted on them such heartless tyranny and injury. History will show that on that day, at the village of Straide, was the beginning of the end of landlordism in Ireland. The Davitt family after eviction crossed to England to seek a living and Michael, as a boy of twelve, was obliged to work in a factory to help his family. While thus employed, he got caught in the machinery and lost an arm. In his early manhood he joined the Fenian movement which led to his conviction for Treason Felony and imprisonment for years. During those years he endured inhuman treatment. Yet, when at last liberated, he set himself the task of smashing the system of which he and his family had been victims and which had inflicted such rapacious tyranny on the peasantry of Ireland. Soon he was joined by Charles Stewart Parnell then coming into notoriety as leader of the Parliamentary Party. A Land League was inaugurated which appealed immediately to the people and branches were formed all over the country. Large public meetings were organised in every district and from platforms all over the country landlordism was denounced in all the moods and tenses. The people were told first to provide food and clothing for themselves and their families before paying rent and then to pay only as much as they could afford. The landlords formed an association, called the Property Defence Association, and a fight to the finish began, which lasted throughout the next three decades, ending in the complete overthrow of landlordism in Ireland.

The early stages of the fight witnessed the shooting of several landlords and agents, threatening letters and notices, boycotting—a form of local ostracism—and wholesale evictions for non-payment of rent. The police force was increased and at one time consisted of 14,000 officers and men. In addition, the Government arranged to employ a number of army reserve men to assist the police on protection duty. These were housed in police barracks and were to have worn a uniform similar to that of the police. Owing, however, to a strong feeling in the Force against having these men placed in the same category as themselves, a distinction by white facings was made in the uniform of the auxiliaries, and Irish wit immediately christened them "the magpies". They failed absolutely to live under the rigid discipline of the R.I.C. and were dismissed one after another, only one man being admitted into the permanent Force as a Constable.

The Land League erected huts for many of the evicted near their old homesteads and sustained them in that position pending a settlement and reinstatement; others of the evicted were afforded temporary accommodation by relations. The Property Defence Association employed men in northern counties—a low type of Orangemen—to assist at evictions, caretake evicted farms and to work for boycotted individuals. These were known as the "emergency men".

Notwithstanding Coercion Acts creating new offences and the suppression of the Land League and National League, which took the place of the former, the agitation continued unabated. Money continued without stint to come into the coffers of the movement, not only from the people of the homeland but from their exiled brethren in America, Australia and Britain. Evictions and prosecutions multiplied. The entire Parliamentary Party, with Parnell at their head, entered into the struggle with all their strength and many of them were prosecuted and imprisoned. Under the Gladstone Government of 1880, Mr W. E. Forster was appointed Chief

Secretary to the Lord Lieutenant. It was he who had recourse to supplying the police with buckshot to fire on the people at short range instead of bullets and made the claim that in doing so he was actuated by humanity, as it was not a deadly means of dispersing illegal assemblies; but at close range, buckshot was quite as deadly, if not more so, than bullets. For this act of humanity, he was known afterwards as "Buckshot Forster". Even buckshot did not stay the people in their march and, as a last resort, he jailed without trial Parnell and the majority of the Parliamentary Party, as well as many others who had been prominent in the agitation.

So intense did the struggle become that the Castle was unable to contend with it. Cartloads of police reports snowed the officials under every morning, with which they were utterly unable to deal. These consisted of shootings, threatening letters and notices posted up in public places and on evicted farms, with crossbones, skull and coffin, and other devices to terrorise. Divisional Commissioners, who had been stipendiary magistrates or police officers, were appointed to the charge of fixed areas in the provinces and all agrarian and political matters delegated to them, each being supplied with a staff officer and clerks, thus relieving the Castle of the burden. A Crime Special Branch was formed, with its head office in the Castle. The work of this Branch was to get in touch with sources of information in relation to secret societies of a revolutionary as well as agrarian character. A man was specially appointed in each district and town, and this was his job, as well as to note the movements of prominent agitators. This man kept a diary in which he recorded the movements of leaders coming under his notice. If a railway station was within his district, he attended the arrival and departure of all passenger trains to watch for the coming and going of suspects, of whom he had a list. When one of them left by train, he had little difficulty in ascertaining his destination and wired in cipher to the police there. The suspect was taken up on arrival, his movements noted and his departure wired to the next halting place. Members of Parliament as well as secret society and other prominent leaders were subjected to this system of "shadowing". The shadowed were quite aware of the fact and often played "hide and seek" with the special men, leaving them in a quandary.

Men were taken up to the Depot and schooled in shorthand, so that in time the police shorthand note taker was found on the platform of every public meeting. One of the crimes usually preferred against leaders was conspiracy, a very subtle and comprehensive charge. It takes two or more to form a conspiracy. Leaders seen together were noted and a record kept. A speech made at a public meeting was recorded by the shorthand note taker. When a sufficient number of "incidents" could be linked together of meetings and movements and speeches, a charge of conspiracy in connection with some offence committed was launched against men, regarding whom evidence had been built up. It might have been a matter in connection with an evicted farm, damages to property or person, intimidation, or some other form of offence, for the commission of which there was no direct evidence; but acts and speeches which could be construed as bearing upon and contributing to the commission of the crime, could be given in evidence. The men charged were tried by two Stipendiary Magistrates. Under the various Coercion Acts, two of those magistrates, certified by the Lord Lieutenant to have sufficient legal knowledge fitting them to try such cases, were appointed for that work. Stipendiary magistrates were appointed by the Government to sit with local justices in Petty Sessions or independently. They were regarded as men prepared to carry out the behests of the Government and were known as "Removeables", meaning that they were not independent and could be removed from their position at any time. They were appointed through influence and generally had been R.I.C. officers, army officers, and needy gentlemen. Thus, for thirty years, the country was the scene of conflict between the people and the Government—the people revolting, the Government repressing—bodies of police moving here and there by rail and car to evictions, public meetings, arrests, trials, etc. The cost of the whole thing should have gone far in buying out all the land of the country.

A Ladies' Land League, as an auxiliary to the principal League, was formed by Miss Anna Parnell and others. They brought assistance to evicted families and prisoners, and otherwise engaged actively in the movement. An effort to render the police unpopular and have them boycotted failed. Young women were warned not to associate with them. This was an even greater failure than in the matter of food and other necessities. Although some young women were invited by parties of men and had their hair forcibly cropped for violating the proscription, absolute failure was the result. Some of the principal members married policemen and of course were struck off the rolls.

In 1881, Gladstone determined on a course of appeasement and Parnell and all the "suspects" in prisons were liberated. He then brought forward and passed a generous Land Act, embracing the three Fs—Fair Rents, Fixity of Tenure, and Free Sale. This measure was well received in the country. The three Fs had been the goal demanded from hundreds of platforms. Mr Forster and Earl Cowper resigned. Earl Spencer became Lord Lieutenant and Lord Frederick Cavendish Chief Secretary. On the day of his arrival in Dublin, 6 May 1882, Lord Cavendish and Mr Burke, Under Secretary, were assassinated in the Phoenix Park on their way to the Vice-Regal Lodge, by members of a secret society, titled "Invincibles". This crime played into the hands of the landlords and was a serious blow to the constitutional movement, which the Parliamentary Party had led so far. Another Coercion Act followed as a matter of course. My object is not to write a history but merely to touch on events to show the difficulties the R.I.C. had to contend with. The conflict continued unabated; Home Rule and Land Purchase being next urged by the Parliamentary Party which, with eighty-five Members in the House of Commons, was in a position to play the two English parties one against the other.

It would indeed be difficult to convey to those who had not lived through that time as a policeman, anything approaching a clear idea of the work imposed on the police during the Land War. As we have seen, previous to 1879, the duties of the Force were neither stringent nor disagreeable and, instead of looking for trouble, the police troubled themselves as little as possible. Their presence was sufficient in most parts of Ireland to maintain order. The Land War changed completely those conditions. Day by day the duties of the police varied and multiplied. Evicted farms had to be kept under observation to detect trespass by former tenants or interference with anyone who might have got possession, either to reside or graze cattle upon them; people who had become unpopular, such as landlords, agents, bailiffs, emergency men, and others who had taken a prominent part on the landlord side had to be protected either by personal guard or vigilant patrolling of their residences and property; arrests and escorts of prisoners, trials at Special Courts and Assizes, attending public meetings to preserve the peace, or to prevent the holding of meetings which had been banned by proclamation: these and many other matters, arising daily, had to receive attention. Then there was constant general patrolling and ambushing by two or more men at all times, day and night, to observe and gather information and detect offenders.

Patrolling was carried out systematically but varied in order to throw intending depredators off guard. The members of the patrol would not always leave the barracks at the same time but in some instances would leave separately, meeting some distance away and getting off roads and passing through fields, or by circuitous ways, and getting into ambush. On other occasions, while a patrol would openly leave a locality and return to barracks, another patrol which had got there unobserved if possible would get into ambush near the place vacated by the previous patrol. In disturbed districts, this special system was arranged by the District Inspector. The Head Constable or Sergeant in charge of the station would beforehand be furnished with a list of patrols to be carried out and, where strict secrecy was to be observed, these instructions were enclosed in a sealed envelope and not opened until the patrol was about to leave the station. These and all other patrols were liable to be visited at uncertain times and places by a District Inspector or Head Constable to see that they were carried out in accordance with instructions.

Individuals receiving personal protection accommodated the guard in or near their residence, the guard supplying their own food. These people were accompanied by the guard wherever they went and, if to a distance by car, followed closely by the guard in another car. Cars were horse-drawn at the time. Protection by patrol was a big responsibility for the police but personal protection was much greater and any remissness in carrying it out would be regarded as a serious dereliction of duty. These people were not always accommodating and obliging toward the guard. They disliked having two policemen following them around and often they would slip away from their houses, through their farms or other places where they thought they were safe, without acquainting the guard, thus placing them, perhaps, in an awkward position. Their attitude toward the men was often churlish and anything but friendly. This attitude was of small account when compared with the cheek and audacity of the "emergency" tribe. These reptiles, instead of gratitude to the police for preserving their hides from being holed, would repay them with impudence and let them understand that it was their job to attend to people rendering service to the State such as theirs. The helpless police had to bear with it all.

Then there was a system of "meet patrols" between adjacent stations, with the object of discussing conditions in adjoining districts, so that men might have information of matters outside their district. The men, however, bothered very little about the idea at the back of these patrols and discussed anything and everything else. Red tape was rampant at the time and these meetings generally afforded a good opportunity for police gossip and what was known as a "good grind"—cutting the socks of all and sundry inside and outside the service.

There was, besides, a class of patrols known as "Rising Patrols". These were an old institution in the service. Rising patrols meant men getting out of bed during the night and remaining on patrol for three or four hours. Needless to say this was not a very inviting turn. A number of these patrols had to be carried out in town and county. Their chief purpose was to watch for evil doers in towns and villages but as a rule were of little value; and men usually got into a quiet and if need be sheltered position and longed for the time when they might return to barracks and to bed.

All patrols were recorded by the senior of the patrol in a book, showing the time absent, places visited, place and time ambushed if any, and anything particular that came under notice, the condition of weather and light if the patrol took place at night. The condition of the night might be useful as evidence in any inquiry. The entry was signed by all the men on the patrol.

From the ordinary duties of three or four hours daily in cities and towns, and occasionally patrolling along the roads in rural areas, men were now required to do at least eight hours daily of exacting hateful work, without the least compensation or consideration beyond defending them in the House of Commons against complaints by the Irish Party. It was a sorry education it is true; men lived in the hope of seeing the end of the trouble but it was hope deferred for a generation.

CHAPTER THIRTEEN.

HOW SERVICE AFFECTED THE MEN.

It may by truly stated that service in the R.I.C. meant living under conditions tending to stamp out every vestige of manhood. Men were obliged to be pliant tools and hypocrites, carrying out orders and duties, many of which were repugnant to the great majority of the service. They were ruled by officers, principally anti-Irish, anti-national, and bigoted, holding nothing in common with the great majority of the men in the ranks and did not consider that any treatment at their hands should be cause for complaint. Realising how much their outlook in the service depended on those officers, men had always to assume willing compliance with them and an unruffled attitude, not alone in carrying out galling orders and duties, but also in adopting a slavish demeanour in their presence. Not only the officers of the Force but the principal Government officials and prominent member of the Ascendancy looked out for that subservient recognition by members of the service and expected salutes and special attention as well as the officers.

In every military force respect by subordinates towards their superiors is essential, and saluting their officers is not felt in any way degrading. But in the R.I.C. the practice was humiliating. It was regarded more as a token of absolute respect for the individual rather than a disciplinary need and some were careful to see that the salute was given, not in a careless matter of form fashion but in correct military style, so that its importance should not suffer in the minds of men. On one occasion within the writer's knowledge, a Head Constable saluted his officer when passing him in the town where both were stationed. The officer signalled the Head Constable into an archway. "Did you want to speak to me Head Constable?" queried the officer. "No sir". "Oh, I thought you did by the way you beckoned me". The Head Constable's salute was not perhaps in the approved form or, more likely, given without sign of trepidation at the approach of his superior. Some of those gentlemen expected that their sudden appearance should give something equivalent to an electric shock to their subordinates and that they should stand in awe before them. It must, however, be stated that this officer was outstanding in his supercilious treatment of subordinates and is not to be taken as an example of the general body of officers. From a disciplinary point of view saluting is not objectionable and should be done smartly and correctly if at all, but in the R.I.C.—not as in a military force—it was part and parcel of the general subservience to which the rank and file were reduced, and men felt it as such.

Besides all this, these men were required to salute ordinary justices of the peace who were met at every street corner. Most of them were of the ordinary respectable community but not entitled to any more nor perhaps as much respect as their neighbours without magisterial status. Then legal officialdom, petty magnates, landlords, their agents, and the entire category of Ascendancy looked out for attention and salutes, whether entitled to them or not. Men could not, therefore, get away from the feeling of subservience inside and outside the service. Yet in their own interest, they were obliged not to show any sign of such feeling but rather that they were pleased with it all. They had not only to keep in view their chances of promotion but many other matters that might affect them. Men were liable to be transferred from station to station and from county to county. Some stations were more desirable that others, especially for married men. Such changes rested as a rule with the officers. Again, any privileges sought should pass through the officers whose recommendation would be needed.

Should trouble come men's way—and no man was immune from it—a helping hand from his officer might mean a lot. In many ways, then, it was necessary that men should stand well with their officers; and well-conducted intelligent men were as a rule able to do so.

What was the effect of all this influence pressing constantly on the character of men is a question which naturally stands out. Well, instead of detracting from, it only added to the strength and virility of their manhood. The grind of discipline had made them quite familiar with the regulations and their rights in the service and, so long as men conformed with the regulations, they could be quite independent, inasmuch as that no advantage could be taken of them. The regulations contained nothing tending to demoralise or sap the character of men but instead fixed a high standard of rectitude to be followed. If, then, men were obliged to live under conditions at variance with the regulations, it only created a feeling of resentment and contributed more and more to the latent strength of their manhood and especially so when that feeling had to be kept in subjection.

The R.I.C. was a proud Force, and they felt it all the more having to exist in an atmosphere tending so much to smother their natural feelings. *Esprit de corps*, not found to the same extent in any other police force, was characteristic of the R.I.C. The members were never known to accept a bribe or money for service rendered to individuals. Once, an Englishman touring the country with a horse and trap—long before the motor car arrived—when passing through a village asked a Constable to hold his horse while he made a short stay, offering him at the same time half-a-crown. The Constable refused to take the money. The Englishman, a little surprised, said "perhaps it is not sufficient". "No", said the Constable "it is not that; if you offered me a sovereign I would not hold your horse, but I'll get a boy to do it for less than half of what you have offered me": and this by a young Constable in the wilds of Erris, in 1875. Of course there were mean flunkeys in the service—no service is without them—but if a man was known to be in the habit of doing mean acts, the other men of the station would not fraternise with him in their pastimes. Accepting free drinks from civilians was regarded as mean and men in the habit of doing so were regarded as unworthy of the reputation of the Force in this respect. In the matter of social drink, they were Irish of the Irish and, to the last call, it was "the same again"—a call by the way which never troubles an Englishman!

Recruited chiefly from the Catholic peasantry, the R.I.C. had received but an elementary education at the National Schools. They, however, got a good Catholic training in their homes and as young men carried that training into the Force. Most of them had never been away from home until they entered the service and were unspoiled country boys. One remarkable feature in the Force was the complete freedom men had to practise their religion. In fact, it was imperative for men to attend Mass on Sunday and they had always to march in a body to and from the church. There was nothing in the service to interfere in the smallest degree with men becoming even better in religion than before they entered; and indeed many of them did become better. Where there were religious sodalities, Catholic police of the place usually had their own guilds. Their attendances at missions and other devotions, though voluntary, was assiduous. Throughout their entire service, their youthful training held them straight and strong in their course and they were remarkable for the great virtues of honesty and morality.

They were noted for their generosity towards every Catholic call. A usual method of raising funds for the erection and renovation of churches and convents was the holding of bazaars. Every R.I.C. station had posted to it a supply of tickets which, as a rule, were never thrown aside but always bought. At Ballycastle, County Antrim, the high altar in the Catholic church, erected alone by the R.I.C., stands there as a memorial to their generosity. Even towards other charitable appeals they were always ready to help. A notable instance once occurred at an eviction when the people assembled made up a subscription to pay the demand by the sheriff, and the police on duty subscribed readily and generously, saving the poor people from being cast on the roadside. Their generosity was so well known that even tramps on the road usually called at wayside stations, and got a helping hand to the next milestone or two. Service in the R.I.C. did not then impair their religion or change their Irish hearts to an appeal for help. They were regarded as "good fellows".

To their people at home, they were always helpful with money if needed and many of the old homesteads might have passed into other hands had it not been for the generosity of the boys in the R.I.C. It can be said of them, too, that they were the best of husbands and fathers. They reared and educated their children to the limits of their means. Their spare time was spent in their homes, helping their wives and doing some useful work for the benefit of the family. Their houses were always as clean and comfortable as possible, and their children well cared for. In after years, wherever fortune placed them, their children acquitted themselves equally well with others of their class. Many of them became priests and nuns and, in one or two instances, bishops; teachers, civil servants, banks, business and other respectable positions they were found filling with credit; but remarkably few of them joined the R.I.C. These are some of the characteristics which go to make up a decent man and the R.I.C. was noted for them all.

In every county in Ireland and especially in the southern and western counties, the Force was connected to a considerable extent, either directly or by marriage, with the families of the people and, taken as a body, they were regarded by all classes as decent men. As bachelors, they were most popular with the fair sex and considered eligible husbands for the daughters of middle class families. They were not as a rule fortune hunters but married the girl of their choice and their married lives were usually happy. As pensioners, they settled down as respectable citizens of their country—an assertion which will hardly be questioned.

It may be urged that, though in the early stages of the
Force, men were ignorant of the nature of the service in
which they enlisted, the political and agrarian movements
should have been an education for the youth of the country
yet, during all that struggle, there was an ample supply of
recruits obtainable. Such a view may be advanced with some
force and is worthy of discussion.

The Parliamentary Party, led by Parnell, aimed first at
getting the land question out of the way before tackling Home
Rule. On the agrarian question then the might of the people
was concentrated. No one conceived that the struggle would
continue for a generation. The "three Fs" was the ultimate
goal aimed at. This gained, the people would settle down and
be quite happy. But, having gained so much, it was seen that
nothing short of purchase of the landlords' interests would
bring peace and contentment to the country. It must be
remembered that during the protracted struggle many of the
methods adopted did not always meet with the approval of the
general public. The Church condemned many things that
happened; throughout, the police were not unpopular. Their
duties no doubt often brought them into conflict with the
people but the general public realised their difficult position
and there was no serious ill-feeling towards them. They were
constantly moving about in bodies, scattering money around
wherever they went, and moved among the people in the
usual friendly way. Any attempt made to boycott them was an
utter failure. With the members of the various Leagues they
were always on good terms. Even members of the Land
League continued to join the Force until the Government
banned their admission. Young men whose families were
connected with the League were not to be recommended, yet
there were instances where the local police "chanced their
arm" and passed through boys on the black list. The fact is
that in all circumstances the R.I.C. were never regarded as
inimical to the people and remained throughout a popular
body during the Land War. Everybody, even Land Leaguers,
realised the need for police and what Force could be found

preferable to the R.I.C.? They were it is true subjected to hard knocks from platforms but they could not and did not expect anything else, when all and sundry in the opposite camp were castigated without limit. Michael Davitt referred to them as mercenaries in their own country. Yet, in his *Fall of Feudalism in Ireland*, he states that the League received valuable information that must have come from members of the Force. He reproduces in the book the cipher method of official communication and confidential orders to the Force. On the occasion of a trial of leading members of the League for conspiracy, regarded as of State importance, he states: "minor officials, under a corrupt government, are not all immaculate and sometimes men who are driven by temptation or poverty to take a hated service under their country's alien rulers retain a sense of sympathetic loyalty to a national cause, which will prompt them to render it assistance in an emergency if possible. The League received many valuable services of this kind in its stormy career."

Thomas Brennan, one of the most brilliant and popular of platform speakers, was not so hurtful as Davitt. At a meeting at Balla, addressing the police on duty, he said he "doubted not that under a dark green jacket there beat many an Irish heart" and appealed to them to throw in their lot with the people. He was one of the traversers arraigned as above and part of the indictment was endeavouring to dissuade the R.I.C. from their allegiance. Parnell himself did not at any time that I remember say anything reflecting on the police.

The R.I.C. might have settled the land question very quickly by throwing down their arms; but, while individuals might resign, anything like a general movement could not be carried out. Stationed in small bodies all over the country, combined action was impossible. The authorities would immediately become aware of it and dismissal of the principal movers would at once put an end to any such attempt. While single men might resign in numbers, it was impossible for married men to do so. Gaps made by individual resignations could have been filled by auxiliaries of one sort or another—

Englishmen, ex-soldiers, Orangemen—and would these have been an improvement on the R.I.C.? It is easy to conceive an effective course of getting over difficulties but to carry it through to success is often the trouble. Again, the R.I.C. had daily experience of the insincerity of many engaged in the agitation. People of no account became local leaders and platform spouters, self being the chief idea at the back of their minds. It is noticeable that in every public movement for the redress of grievances people come to the front as strong supporters of the cause but are actuated solely by the view that something would come out of the whole thing to their own advantage. The Land League, the National League, and every other league were full of such people. During the Plan of Campaign to pay no rent, if a reasonable offer was refused, it was known that people who had been prominent advocates of the Plan had sneaked into the rent offices behind the backs of their fellows and paid their rents.

This selfishness was not confined to the ordinary class of the people. As an example, we need only recall the Parnellite split. Here we saw a condition of things arising that divided the people and kept them divided for ten years, their leaders hurling opprobrious imputations at one another, while the interests of the country remained in abeyance. Was it patriotic unselfishness that actuated those men to carry on that bitter, senseless, disintegrating campaign to the delight of the English Government and the enemies of the country, as Ireland did not trouble them as long as the row continued? Is it not then reasonable to assume that patriotic, unselfish men would have sunk their private feelings and come together, instead of doing their utmost to create bad blood and intensify the conditions which existed during the regrettable period?

Many other things might be advanced to show that the R.I.C. had no reason to think they were regarded with disfavour by the people who to a great extent had become reconciled to English rule if justly treated. This was seen in the extraordinary reception given King Edward and his Queen on their visit here in July 1903, when they made their way through cheering crowds and beflagged Dublin, from Kingstown to the Vice-Regal Lodge in the Phoenix Park, where deputations from various parts of the country awaited to present them with addresses of welcome; and wherever the King went to see for himself and hear from the people their wants, he was received with enthusiasm. It was known that King Edward was friendly towards Ireland and that Ireland should be ruled, not by coercion, but in accordance "with Irish ideas".

Another aspect of the R.I.C. is deserving of consideration. Let it be supposed that the country had been policed by Englishmen and nondescripts instead of Irishmen, would it have been preferable or any more to the advantage of the country? During its existence, probably 80,000 Irishmen joined and served in the Force until pensioned. If these men had not joined the R.I.C., most of them certainly would have emigrated. Seventy thousand of them at least married 70,000 Irish girls, many of whom, too, would have settled in other countries. These men and women reared families averaging five or six children each and on the whole contributed to the population of the country, probably half a million people. Their salaries and pensions were spent in the country. Their children were as Irish, *even more so than the majority*. What they had heard from their fathers and mothers in the family circle of the conditions that ruled in the service implanted in them a virile Catholic spirit and a hatred of English rule. During the Anglo-Irish conflict, R.I.C. pensioners' children—boys and girls—were amongst the most active in fighting and aiding in many ways the Irish cause. In the serving ranks too, the Republicans had plenty of friends. They detested the cruel position in which they were placed by being obliged to accompany the Auxiliaries, and Blacks and Tans on their murderous raiding expeditions but were, if possible, a restraint upon them and may have often saved the lives of people by privately communicating projected raids. The writer has personal knowledge of a District Inspector preventing the destruction of a creamery by Black and Tans, and the wrecking by them of a small town in the vicinity of which two policemen had been shot dead.

Rather than remaining in command of the R.I.C., if
employed in the execution of methods intended by the
Government for the suppression of the rebellion, Sir Joseph
Byrne, the last of the R.I.C. Inspectors General, resigned and
that Force henceforth came under military control. Small
parties at outlying stations which were being attacked by Sinn
Féiners were moved to large centres. They received instructions to accompany the regular military, Auxiliaries and Black
and Tans when required on their raiding and lorry excursions
through the country, but those forces had a free hand and
could go raiding on their own account and it was on such
occasions that shootings and burnings and lootings generally
occurred. They preferred to be without the R.I.C. on such
occasions. Lloyd George dressed the Auxiliaries in R.I.C.
uniform to do work he knew the R.I.C. would not do and, if
public complaint reached the House of Commons of the
outrages committed by these disguised military marauders, he
could answer they were merely "police measures".

R.I.C. resignations began to pour into Dublin Castle.
Arthur Griffith on one occasion stated that a thousand men
had resigned and that many more were prepared to go if they
could see their way out but that he was unable to give them
any guarantee.

At Listowel, County Kerry on 17 June 1920, a historic
incident occurred. Ambushes by the Republican forces had
been inflicting losses on the English who at the time might be
regarded as on the defensive. The English Command prepared
to take more active measures. A Colonel Smyth, Divisional
Police Commissioner for Munster, was despatched to police
stations to instruct the men on the new idea. In future, they
were told not to wait until fired upon but to get into ambush
and when people came along with hands in pockets or under
suspicious circumstances to shout "hands up" and if they did
not immediately comply to shoot, and with effect. The police
were informed that any man not prepared to carry out these
instructions could resign—that there was no need for him.
The Listowel police had information of Smyth's coming and

the purpose of it. They discussed among themselves what their attitude should be and appointed a Constable as spokesman for the party. In due course Smyth accompanied by other officers arrived. The men were assembled in the dayroom and the Colonel explained the new plan of campaign. He proceeded to put the question individually to the men but was told that Constable Mee[1] would answer for them. "That means", said Constable Mee, "that we are to shoot at sight. I presume you are an Englishman, but you seem to forget that you are talking to Irishmen. These, too, are English, and you can have them", taking off his belt and side arms and pitching them on the table. "You are a murderer and to hell with you", and with the party walked out of the room. A month afterwards Smyth was shot by I.R.A. men who entered and found him in the Country Club, Cork city.[2]

Constable Mee and fourteen other Constables resigned. District Inspector Flanagan [R.I.C. 53949] who had charge of the Listowel party stood by the men in their action and, in consequence, was retired on a Sergeant's pension after twenty-three years' service. It may be of interest here to state that District Inspector Flanagan and his clerk, Constable Hughes [R.I.C. 66270], both became missionary priests and the latter is now a bishop in Nigeria. Constable Mee, the leader of the revolt, joined the Republican forces and served with them until the end of the conflict. Needless to say, there was a keen outlook for him by the Crown forces and, when they failed to lay hands upon him, they wreaked their vengeance upon his family. On 17 May 1921, four lorry loads of Auxiliaries and Black and Tans drove to his father's house and, in the depth of the night, broke into it and demanded from Mr. Mee the address of his son, Jeremiah and, when this

---

1 Jeremiah Mee (R.I.C. 65466). His memoir has been published by J. Anthony Gaughan, *Memoirs of Constable Jeremiah Mee, R.I.C.* (Dublin: Anvil Press, 1975).
2 Gerald Bryce Ferguson Smyth, who does not appear to have had an R.I.C. number, was killed on 17 July 1920.

information was not given to them, ordered the family consisting of Mr. Mee, his wife, and two daughters, seventeen and
eighteen years of age, out of the house in their night attire,
without giving them time to dress decently and lined them up
against a wall under an armed guard. With a supply of petrol,
they then set fire to the dwelling house and out offices, hay,
oats, carts, harness and farming implements, burning everything
to ashes and, during two hours of this destruction, Mr. and Mrs.
Mee and their two young girls were kept standing in their
night dresses under an armed guard of brutal marauders—
soldiers would surely be a misnomer! A more cruel and
cowardly outrage would be difficult to conceive; and what
for?—because Jeremiah Mee would not deliver up his gallant
son to his would-be assassins.

The Government saw the possible danger of a general
revolt of the R.I.C. had the project of shooting people before
they had time to explain their presence been persisted with,
and the shooting-at-sight stunt came to an end. The R.I.C.
were not out at any time for wanton destruction of life and
property. Their whole being and natural instincts recoiled
from such crimes and though 150 of them had been killed in
ambush attacks and otherwise from vantage positions, they
had no recourse to reprisals, ill-treatment, or shooting their
prisoners "trying to escape"; only in self defence, when
attacked by armed parties, did they use their arms.

The one terrible stain on the R.I.C. was the murder of
Thomas MacCurtain, Lord Mayor of Cork. There cannot be
any doubt but that crime was committed by members of the
city police as a reprisal. A short time previously a District
Inspector and Head Constable, while passing through the
principal street of the city, were fired at, the District Inspector
having been seriously wounded. A few days afterwards, a
Constable on patrol duty on the outskirts of the city was shot
and a few hours before the Lord Mayor was murdered,
another Constable passing along the quays to his lodgings was
shot dead. There is no need to discuss the pros and cons of the
murder of the Lord Mayor which were raised at the time and

since. All the evidence pointed to the guilt of the R.I.C; District Inspector Swanzy who was stationed in Cork at the time was shot in Lisburn to which town he had been transferred.[3]

In other instances in which the R.I.C. were accused of reprisals there was no convincing evidence of their guilt. The R.I.C. was accused of supplying the Crown forces with information and guiding them to the houses of Sinn Féiners. Individual members may have done so on their own account but otherwise the general body detested association with these forces and rendered them no assistance in their depredatory expeditions; in fact the people felt that the presence of the members of the R.I.C. meant more security for them. Outside the R.I.C. all the Crown forces had many sources of information; *and not all the spies* were found dead and labelled "spies beware". While the majority of the people were in sympathy with the Sinn Féiners and afforded them all the help possible, without bringing them under notice, there were others—and these were not confined to one section—who supplied the Crown forces with information as to the residences of Sinn Féiners and their movements. Sinn Féiners, when resting in houses and other places, found themselves surrounded by Crown forces who raced to the place in lorries and wiped them out! Someone, as at Clonmult, had conveyed to the nearest military post the information. It was not in the R.I.C. the spies were to be found but among the class who regarded the outbreak as a crime against the country, as well as in a lower order of the community in the hope of gain, sinister petty malice, or other motive.

With law and order cast to the winds, a censored Press, and the country in a state of confusion, the historian of the future will have difficulty, without any reliable record, in giving in detail a clear account of all that occurred in that eventful period of Irish history. Of those who lived through and witnessed that conflict, a majority still exist; and the R.I.C. I

3 Oswald Ross Swanzy (R.I.C. 61367) was killed on 22 August 1920.

believe can now confidently appeal to that majority that during that period of trial for themselves, as well as for the people, they avoided, as far as possible, any action involving the destruction of life or property.

CHAPTER FOURTEEN.

DISCIPLINARY RESTRAINT.

Under the conditions outlined in the preceding chapters it is unnecessary to say that Catholic members of the Force required to be careful to avoid anything in speech or action which would indicate that they held views different to the spirit that ruled in the service. Constant care in this respect had, however, enabled men without embarrassment to cloak their private feelings, giving no inkling of what was at the back of their minds. For anyone who hoped to advance in the service, it was incumbent upon him to guard against even suspicion of holding any views not in conformity with those of the people in whose hands rested his advance. The only member of the rank and file who could afford, to a great extent, to be independent of the private views of others was a Head Constable who did not ambition promotion, or who had become ineligible for it through age or other cause. Most Head Constables had a good knowledge of the regulations and their experience enabled them to shoulder the responsibilities of the rank, with less difficulty and worry than lay in their path up to the time they had gained that position. A Head Constable, while responsible for the discipline and supervision of the duties of his station, had the assistance of the Sergeants in ordinary matters and the District Inspector at hand to consult in any difficulty. He was not obliged to be a martinet and could safely exercise sound discretion in the treatment of his subordinates.

Notwithstanding their stringency, a narrow interpretation of the regulations was not desired by the higher authorities. Prestige alone gained in the minds of men by his own conduct enabled a Head Constable to rule his subordinates more effectively than by holding the regulations as a whip over their heads every day of their lives. When men felt that they were being treated in a just and generous fashion and that no advantage would be taken of them for mere shortcomings, they, as a rule, responded willingly, without any recourse to rules or regulations. The Head Constable was closely associated with the District Inspector in the general work of the station and, where a clerk was not supplied to him, the Head Constable assisted the District Inspector in his office work. As a rule, the Head Constables and District Inspectors got on well together but there were some exceptions where the relations between them were anything but happy. In such instances, a weak Head Constable sought the line of least resistance, but a competent Head Constable could well afford to stand up against treatment tending to degrade him in his position or reduce his authority in the eyes of his subordinates. A few instances, of which I had personal knowledge, will serve as an example of the latent spirit in the service, which men were obliged to keep in subjection.

During the Land War, public meetings were frequently banned by proclamation. It was necessary in such instances to have an information sworn by a member of the Force that the holding of such a meeting would have the effect of causing fear and alarm in the minds of Her Majesty's subjects, or which was likely to cause a disturbance of the peace, or the object of which was to intimidate people from exercising their lawful rights, or some other ground. On one occasion, the District Inspector and the Resident Stipendiary Magistrate had prepared the necessary information for submission to the Castle to justify the banning of a meeting. The Head Constable was called into the District Inspector's office and a Testament was handed to him by the Magistrate requiring him to swear to the information they had prepared. Pitching the Testament out of his hand, "No; I am not going to swear to order for anybody" declared the Head Constable, to the amazement of the two officials. The District Inspector himself had to swear the information.

Another instance: on one occasion, religious tracts from a Protestant source arrived at the station through the post. The Head Constable attached a copy to a statement that the men of the station resented having such papers sent to them. It was an unusual course to take official notice of such a matter. The County Inspector asked for the names of the men who had made the affair a cause of complaint, believing the Head Constable would be unable to name anyone. The Head Constable himself replied that *he himself resented the practice*. The fact is that neither the Head Constable nor anyone at the station troubled in the least about the matter. The Head Constable and the District Inspector had not been pulling smoothly together and the Head Constable adopted this means to show the District and County Inspectors—both Protestants—that he was not of the "slave mind" and how indifferent he was as to what they thought of him. Needless to say, he was not out for promotion. The District Inspector was a typical snob, better at giving trouble than anything else.

Another District Inspector had been domineering over the Head Constable. He was a self-sufficient gentleman who would treat a Head Constable with as little consideration as he would a Constable. The District Inspector was not allowed a clerk and the Head Constable assisted him in his office work. In such instances, the regulations required that the Head Constable was not to be employed later than 1 p.m. each day. This regulation, however, remained a dead letter and the Head Constable usually remained in the office until the day's work was finished. In this instance, as soon as the clock struck one, the Head Constable stood up and left the office, leaving the District Inspector to complete the work himself. Correspondence and keeping the cash book was the chief work of the District Inspector. All the drudgery of preparing accounts and returns, keeping the records, copying correspondence, and the entire routine of the office was done by the Head Constable; clerks were allowed only in large centres. This gentleman was very apt in having regulations in other respects strictly enforced. The Head Constable gave him a taste of the same medicine, and with good effect.

Anonymous letters, generally with some personal motive, were often received by the police. The regulations said that such communications might often contain useful information and should not always be ignored. One Head Constable used to post some of them on the notice board and let the public judge their source. This was rather a bold thing for the Head Constable to do on his own account. But it demonstrated to the public that the police were not to be influenced by such methods and this I am sure would have been his explanation if called on for one.

Many other instances I have no doubt could be given to show that a Head Constable could maintain his position without having recourse to methods not imposed on him by regulation, even if his attitude ran counter to the view of a superior officer. It was, however, only in exceptional cases that a Head Constable was obliged to assert himself. As a rule, he and the District Inspector got on well together and in most instances the District Inspector left the control of the station chiefly in the hands of the Head Constable.

CHAPTER FIFTEEN.

A FEW REFLECTIONS.

During the 1870s, landlordism reached the zenith of its power and oppression. All over the land wherever one went, those lords of the soil were found seated in their demesnes, inside the boundary walls of which the public were notified in distinct characters that, "trespassers will be prosecuted according to law"—the law dispensed by themselves and their fellows. Who were those people, how did they get there and, above all, how did they become the practical rulers of the countryside around? Hardly one, I suppose, of those subject to their domination could give a clear answer or any answer at all to those questions. As much as they knew about them was that they or their progenitors had been there as long as they or their fathers had remembered, and had been regarded by them as the owners of the land on which they lived and to whom they had paid rent for the privilege. One cannot blame the people for not knowing more of those exactors of their sweat. They had followed in the footsteps of their fathers who had spent their lives in toil, acknowledging the lordship to which those tyrants laid claim and to question their right was a thing that never once dawned upon them. Into such conditions and servility the people were born, from which they saw no possibility of escape and tried to make the most of their lot. Generation after generation had come and gone, and their children grew up imbibing from their fathers and mothers, and the example of their neighbourhood, a dread of the power held over their lives and the need to stand well with the big house and all connected with it. We cannot wonder then at the slavish spirit of the people, until Parnell came along and told them to stand erect and no longer continue to doff their hats to their oppressors.

Then only did the Irish peasantry begin to feel the blood tingle in their veins and take their place under the standard hoisted by Michael Davitt at Straide. Who could have foreseen the revolution which resulted in the tenure of the soil, from that enterprise of 1879, by the father of the Land League? At most, did the people hope for was some amelioration of their state and, though they set up the three Fs as their ultimate goal, they felt the difficulty of achieving it within measurable time if at all. Yet 1880 had not passed until good headway had been made towards their object. It was only then that the landlords began to feel that their position was not as secure as they had believed. They and their forebears had held sway over the people for 300 years or more. They had been the mainstay of English rule in the country during that time and now they were confident that England was not going to let them down; and so they boldly took up the gauge of battle the Land League had flung down to them. They were not only the mainstay of British rule but also the pillars of the Ascendancy, who had dug themselves in all over the country and to a man were at the back of their benefactors. The accumulation of tyranny and injustice had at last, in the face of world opinion, rendered the aid from England short of that expected. By Coercion Acts, the onslaughts of the people were stayed as far as possible, while by stages legislative reform was conceded until, not alone were the three Fs achieved but also purchase of the landlords' titles.

When one considers the power exercised over the people by those arrogant tyrants with the might of England behind them all those years, such a revolution is comparable only with many that elsewhere cost rivers of blood. A few on both sides fell but on the whole it was a bloodless revolution. With the dethronement of those heartless despoilers of the people came the tottering to its foundations of the Ascendancy.

William O'Brien, who had written of their lost opportunities, would have preferred their remaining here. Michael Davitt would have given them a single ticket to Holyhead. No; they could not think of settling in a land, despised by the people over whom they had wielded such unscrupulous power and so, with few exceptions, they did take single tickets to Holyhead; and of the many who saw them off without regret, the Royal Irish Constabulary were not the least.

Discussing the question with a comrade at the time, I observed that the price given the landlords was too high. "Not at all", he replied, "why do you think so, John?" (that was his name), I queried, "well, the more they'll have the more they'll drink, and the devil will have them all the quicker", he replied. Though I am sure he did not wish that to be their ultimate fate, he sincerely believed they had no claim to heaven. John had been reared on the estate of one of the most notorious, tyrannical landlords. Here is his description of the estate office to which the tenantry repaired to pay their rents. On the path to the office, two mastiff dogs—one at each side—charged out at strangers until checked by their chains, then a swift deep rivulet had to be crossed on narrow planks before reaching the rent office. Two officials sat at a table on which lay two loaded revolvers. Such an experience did not encourage much hope of favours and seldom was one asked; rather in John's words, "the people were glad to get away with whole skins". One can well understand why John rejoiced at the complete turn of fortune's wheel! As honest as the sun, poor John had since crossed the Bourne—peace to his ashes.

As we generally know, their agents were aiders and abettors in the actions of the landlords. They were opposed to reasonable settlements and were dead against purchase. They were constantly at the elbows of their employers tendering cunning advice. During the heat and bitterness of the struggle, many landlords, beside those who were usually absentees, were prevailed upon to live in England for safety. That was the very thing the agents desired, for then they could represent the state of affairs to suit their own purposes and that as a rule had the effect of keeping the landlords out of the way.

I remember one instance where an agent in the absence of his employers had a police hut erected for his own protection at a place known by the landlord as an ideal position for an ambush. There had been no trouble on the estate. Neither the landlord nor the agent was unpopular and not the slightest danger existed to either. The landlord had lived much of his time in England, visiting occasionally his estate. He was a timid, well-disposed man. The erection of a police hut for the protection of his agent put a stop to even occasional visits. It was said that the agent had in view the acquisition of the estate for himself but the hope, if it did exist, did not mature. It was heavily mortgaged and eventually was acquired by the tenantry. A religious order now occupies the mansion, beautifully situated in the midst of spacious gladed woodlands, in one of the most historic spots in Ireland.

House agents as well as land agents availed of the turmoil to bring grist to their own mill. In most towns there was house property inherited by people having their homes abroad. During that trouble, when confiscation was supposed to be rampant in the country, through reports broadcast by the Press, there was little difficulty in getting those people to sell out at a quarter of its value, and the property was bought in the name of another, when actually it was the agent himself who acquired it.

Even in official quarters, people were found to discover, in the heat of battle, a leverage towards promotion. The Castle, in making appointments, kept in view the services rendered by its supporters, whether in or out of the service. Its most efficient and useful supporters were likely to be the more unpopular and to suffer at the hands of the Leaguers. When a job better than that held by an aspirant appeared in the offing, the unpopularity of the aspiring candidate became intensified and he felt the need for increased police protection; and constant patrolling followed about his residence and property. Once the appointment had been gained, police watchfulness gradually ceased and he continued to follow his course through life unmolested.

Always and even today the English Press has been the constant enemy of Ireland, and so it was during the Land War. Every occurrence that could be used to poison the minds of the English people towards the Irish people was exaggerated or distorted without restraint. Here is an instance for example: letting grasslands, on what was known as the eleven months' system, was opposed by the Land League. The eleven months' system enabled the owner to let the land for eleven months to the highest bidder and thus was an obstacle to having the land divided among the people. In this instance, twelve cattle which had been placed on a field hired for eleven months died immediately of poisoning, caused by the animals licking white lead found in small tubs in the field. At once, the outrage was attributed to the Land League. The English Press rang, in its highest notes, of the barbarity to which the Irish people had sunk, and was aided to the full by the Ascendancy here who regarded the affair as a telling occurrence to damage the reputation of the League. The owner of the cattle sought compensation under the Malicious Injury Act. The County Council opposed the application but, notwithstanding the evidence of the police that the tubs had evidently been in the field long before the cattle had been placed there, since it was seen that young grass had grown around the vessels and that the soil underneath them was bare, the County Court Judge granted compensation, thus holding that the occurrence was a malicious act. The County Council appealed the case. The decision of the lower court was reversed at Assizes and the case dismissed on the evidence of the police.

A remarkable feature to the discredit of the people was revealed in connection with this case. In the time that elapsed between the trial at the County Sessions and Assizes, the police tried to discover how the vessels containing the white lead had got into the field but it was only after the case had been disposed of at the Assizes that they learned of it. The field was close by a railway station, a low wall separating it from the engine shed. White lead was used by the railway men in connection with the engines. The tubs containing the lead had not been emptied to the bottom and, as fresh supplies were taken into use, were rolled down the embankment, and remained on the railway side of the wall separating the railway premises from the field. Boys came along to kick football in the field and, finding the tubs on the other side of the wall, took them into the field to serve as goal posts, and left them there where they remained unnoticed until the cattle had been poisoned.

Here is an instance where the reputation of a community was assailed far and near, in the most malignant fashion and, though it was well known how the tubs got into the field, not an individual of the community came forward to tell the police how the thing happened. This was a case appealing to the people to assist the police to establish the truth but they remained dumb in the face of the lying imputation. Nor did the result of this notorious incident ever appear outside the locality where it happened! It is a sad instance of the want of public spirit and duty, too common in the country. British rule we know engendered in the minds of the people a deter-mination not to assist the authorities in the administration of the law, but this was not a matter to be regarded from that viewpoint; and the only reason that could be assigned for their silence was that no one wished to be the means of standing in the way of the owner of the cattle receiving compensation— a view that should not have been entertained.

The ceilidhe house was the retail shop of the latest news, spiced with plenty of wit and humour. It was in the early days of the Land League. At one of those casual assemblies in a cottage, outside the demesne walls of the landlord of the place, this happened. The League was getting into its stride and was going so well that people began to pluck up and envision better times when landlords would be brought to their knees. On this occasion, the ceilidhers joked about the lord of the soil over the wall and how in due course they would parcel out the lands he held himself, including the demesne and mansion. They played cards for the assignment of the various lots, the tenant of the cottage winning the mansion and demesne, the landlord to be given his cottage. When the story got out, it set the countryside laughing as they retailed it to one another. As well might they think of carving up the moon! Even the gamblers themselves laughed at the idea. Yet, ridiculous as it seemed at the time, that very estate and others as well, including the sacrosanct demesne lands, passed into the hands of the people. It is true, "the mills of God grind slowly, but they grind exceeding small"; and never was this aphorism more fully exemplified than in the abolition of Irish landlordism.

In few countries, perhaps, are found so many features of their history as in Ireland. They are to be seen wherever one goes, telling of barbarity and spoliation, as well as of the virility and unconquerable spirit that saved the race from extinction. The people are not to be blamed if they have known little or nothing of the landmarks, dotting the face of the country everywhere and holding a story to be passed onto the generations. The ruins of castles and mansions, churches and monasteries, of ancient cemeteries, and sites of evictions (grazing ranches) have been little more to the people than mere features of the landscape. Denied education and reduced to a condition of serfdom, in which their safest course was to conform to the will of their masters and not to look back, the story which those ruins told of blood and tears became in time a closed book to the people. In their ignorance, they could not see the value of those records of their past and in many instances damaged further what remained of them, by removing the stonework—often the most important—to build walls and fences, or turn them into cattle sheds. During the writer's service in the R.I.C., because of public complaints of the neglect of the Government in permitting the continued damage to historic ruins, the Board of Works took charge of the most important ones and issued a pamphlet on the subject. That pamphlet was sent to every police station, with instructions to prevent as far as possible damage to those ruins. But in all the schooling with which the Force was saturated, I never once heard the subject mentioned. The preservation of those ruins did not appeal to Dublin Castle, rather would it have seen them blotted from the map and R.I.C. officers knew that they would not be held to account if the Board of Works' pamphlet became dust-covered on the shelf.

The only interest the police had in those historic ruins was if, on a wintry night while on patrol, one was at hand that afforded shelter from storm and rain, advantage might be taken of it. While sheltered from the drifting rain and listening to the drip, drip from some projecting part of the ruin adding to the sadness and desolation of the place, if any one of the party were of a contemplative mood he might picture a night in the dim past when that ruin was a noble pile, shedding brilliant lights on the court-yard and surroundings, and filled with the joy of life by youth and beauty, the vibrations of the harp chords floating out upon the breeze; but, at that moment, his reverie might be suddenly brought to a close by the challenge of a night owl, the sole tenant of that once battle-mented stronghold of a proud chieftain! Such reflections were indeed possible, even to a police patrol, whose chief purpose here might have been to see that all was well with the descendant of some Cromwellian usurper within his walled demesne nearby.

CHAPTER SIXTEEN.

A RETROSPECT OF SEVENTY YEARS.

Only those who have lived through the past seventy or eighty years can have a clear conception of the changes that have taken place in Ireland. Down through the 1860s and 1870s the people had sunk to a condition of servitude probably unequalled elsewhere in Europe, outside of Russia. The futile attempt in 1867 to revolt only confirmed in the minds of the people that the idea to overthrow English rule in this country could only end in disaster to those who made the attempt. Who could think otherwise—an unarmed, ignorant peasantry standing up against a great military power such as England? And so the people had come to accept their position as their lot, without hope, and settled down to make the most of it. Gladstone's Land Act of 1870 brought little change, as the landlords had still power to increase rents and those evicted were poor people who had no claims for improvements, as they had no means to make any. The Home Rule Party elected in 1874, with Mr. Butt as leader, gladdened the hearts of the people but they felt that such a time was not within reasonable distance and did not mind to see it pushed aside to make way for land reform.

Outside Ulster, where the linen industry was very helpful to small farmers whose families engaged in handloom weaving in their homes, the industries which had existed in the smaller towns had disappeared, while those in the cities and larger towns had dwindled and become fewer. The people were, therefore, driven to rely upon the land more and more for existence. Their knowledge of the world was very limited and, though the system of elementary education had been brought within their reach, they did not see the value of it. They could not see any outlook for their children other than manual labour at home or in some other country, and what education did they need more than to be able to read and write a letter without having to depend on another to do it for them? A large portion of the people—thirty or forty per cent—could neither read nor write. To meet the demands of the landlord and to hold on to their homes were the chief concern of the people.

Those were the days of the spade and shovel, sickle and flail, scythe and fork, and men and women, boys and girls, had all to give a helping hand. Except ploughing and harrowing, all work on the land was done by manual labour. Today it would be regarded as a slow process but men were wonderfully proficient in the use of the implements employed— the writer should know, as he handled them all before engaging in a course of physical jerks—and got over the ground quicker than could now be imagined. It was laborious work but it had its advantages. The work was better done with no waste and it gave employment to three or four times as many men, besides boys and girls, as at present. Very much more land was cultivated than now, as the people lived chiefly on the produce of the soil, importing little of anything. If the farm was small, members of the family worked for larger farmers for a small wage and food. As well as the annual harvesting migration, there was a good deal of going and coming to and from England and Scotland of able-bodied young men who were unable to get to America. These always got employment there in the hard and dangerous jobs—coal mines, foundries, shipyards, quarrying, etc. Many of them settled there and their descendants may be found all over in both countries today; others made it a stepping stone on their way to America, when they had saved their passage money. There were no labour unions, no unemployment or insurance benefit, no Workmen's Compensation Act, no old age pensions, no half-holidays.

People had to work or beg. The workhouse was the only other alternative. Many too old or unfitted for work did become inmates of those institutions and lived their lives in them, ending in a pauper's grave. Others preferred to appeal to the charity of the people and begged from house to house for alms which were usually given in bread or foodstuffs; whole families could be seen travelling the roads.

Machinery and English and Scotch competition had not yet affected local trades; and shoemakers, tailors, carpenters, coopers, etc., continued to supply the needs of the people. Even handy men were able to earn a living, especially in towns making and mending household requisites. One of these found in every district deserves mention because he stands out in the history of the time. He was the besom maker, whose handiwork was familiar in the homes of the people. The raw material, in the shape of heather, which he had for the cutting on the bogs and mountain slopes, he fashioned into neat hand besoms, which he retailed from house to house for two or three pence each. He was not an extortionist, but just out to make a living, was in nobody's way in any sense, being usually a little fellow, and had no enemies—just an item that fitted into the life of the community. But the time came when brooms of brent and fibre were dumped on our quays and brushed aside the heather and the besom maker was no longer found on the moor. The fate of the besom makers was the fate of all our crafts and industries, brought about by conditions over which the people had no control.

Street trading at fairs and markets was a feature and standings on the streets, on which tradesmen displayed their work, was customary. Boots, clothing and household requisites were offered for sale. "Cheap Johns" and travelling peddlers were there too, enlivening the place with their ready wit, while disposing of their wares. The travelling fraternity of entertainers was also usually represented. Fairs and races were the chief rendezvous of jugglers, acrobats, ballad singers, punch and judy, and all the others, picking up the loose pennies. In those days fairs combined business and pleasure to a great extent and people, especially young people, went to them for the day's outing. "I hope you're not going to Bandon fair. Indeed I'm not wanting to met you there, impudent Barney O'Hea". This it will be remembered was the sly method adopted by Barney O'Hea's sweetheart of reminding him not to forget coming to the fair; nor did he, for we have it that "As I was going up Bandon Street, just who do you think myself did meet but impudent Barney O'Hea"; and though she bid him that minute to get out of her way, his drollery forced her to laugh; and one day to prevent him killing a rival became Mrs O'Hea. In addition to the variety of the fare contributed by the travelling fraternity, dancing and social intercourse with acquaintance went to the making of a pleasurable outing, and a subject for gossip during the ensuing week. In the limited outlook of country life at the time, youthful spirit was easily satisfied and a day at the fair or any social gathering was enjoyed to the full. One of the sayings at the time of anything amusing was "it was as good as a day at a fair".

One of my earliest recollections was an incident at a fair. I happened to get into a ring where the three card game was being played. It was the first time I had seen the game but I was old enough to understand it. The gamester was ringing the changes in the well-known style. An old farmer, who must have had a good fair, crushed into the ring to see what it was all about. Some were winning, others losing, the winners doubtless being confederates—I have since learned so much. The farmer seemed to think there was no difficulty in turning up the winning card, the queen, for he abused losers for their stupidity. The player moved the cards once more and then turned to sing out to passers-by what they were missing. Immediately a gentleman—a confederate no doubt—close to the board deftly turned up the winning card so that it could be seen, replacing it in an instant. Now there could be no mistake made. Turning to the board again, the player moved the cards slowly a few times, longwise and crosswise, but the farmer thought he had kept a steady eye on the card the gentleman had exposed. No, he could not make a mistake and planked a pound note on the board, that he would turn up the winning card. A pound note was a lot of money then. The player hesitated and made a motion to move the cards again, but the gentleman at the opposite side of the board intervened. "No, the cards would not be moved again until the bet was decided." Accepting the bet, the player took up the pound note. The attention of the crowd became tense as the farmer reached out and turned up—heavens! not the winning queen, but the deuce. The gamester continued to carry on as through nothing had happened, telling the farmer that luck would come his way and to have another try. But the farmer had had enough and slipped out of the crowd. Sensing trouble, the gamester also left, saying he would be back in a few minutes. Soon the farmer returned with two stalwart young fellows carrying ash plants. The board was there but the owner, where was he? The farmer and his boys were told that he had left, saying he would be back in a few minutes. They're waiting for him yet!

Every day except Sundays and religious holidays, which were strictly observed, meant work and a break off for a day was welcomed. In all their tribulations, the characteristic gaiety of the people lived on and, forgetting all their troubles, enjoyed heartily amusements as they came. Their sources of enjoyment were limited, being confined chiefly to their own locality. Athletics of any sort were always an engaging pastime for the youth and occasional competitive meetings took place in local centres. Football was not so extensively played as at present but handball was very popular, and the players attained a high standard of skill at the game. Hurling had completely fallen away, until revived in the middle 1880s. A horse race or a circus was an event not to be missed and crowds of both sexes flocked to them from all sides. The seaside, lakes, the ruins of ancient castles and ecclesiastical institutions, usually set in picturesque surroundings reminiscent of Éire's ancient glory, and other places which, down through the generations, had an attraction for the people. Youth and middle-aged found them a pleasant resort on sunny Sunday and holiday evenings and were a general source of summer-time outing. The Pattern, once a source of amusement as well as religion, was banned by the Church on account of abuses but is being revived under orderly and proper conditions.

The crossroads dance had almost disappeared but fitfully held on in many places. The dance, however, was unsup-pressible for it was in the people's blood; if they ceased to dance, it was Ireland no longer. The travelling fiddler did his part in keeping the dance going and was welcomed in every district. Many of these successors of the harpers were blind but the children vied with one another for the privilege of leading the blind fiddler around. Suitable houses were selected for the dances which were crowded by young and old. Elderly fathers and mothers became young again and took the floor to show the boys and girls that they were not in it with them at the jigs and reels. The hat was always sent round for the fiddler and he had free quarters as long as he remained in the neigh-bourhood. Other small dances, some of them impromptu, when a crowd got together were constantly held. The absence of a musician did not matter. Lilting, accompanied by an improvised cymbal—the fire tongs and a spoon, or something else at hand that would ring out the bars—supplied the music. Lilting was an art cultivated by both men and women and created more merriment than any instrument. By and by, the concertina and melodeon came along, and the blind fiddler and his times passed into song and story; but the few of the period who remain will be heard today sighing out "God be with the good old times".

Children were children then, in every sense of the word and had their games and regulated periods for many of them. The boys had marbles, tops, rolling hoops, kites, handball, and many others; the girls had jackstones, tip cat, skipping, round rings by catching hands, and dancing right and left with sing-songs. Some of the games were played by boys and girls together, such as round rings, hopscotch and blind man's bluff; the tomboys insisted on joining in all the boys' games, and had often to be cuffed out of them. Often the busiest part of a policeman's job on street duty in towns was to prevent boys rolling hoops, playing ball, spinning tops, and the girls skipping, playing jacks, and hopscotch on the footpath; the need for strict regulation of the streets was not so essential at the time nor for years after the motor car came into use, as only the rich could afford the cost. Those innocent games, freely entered into without restraint, brought the body and muscles into action in various positions and not alone made for physical development but contributed to the alertness of the eye and the mind and, generally, were a healthy and enjoyable pastime for children. The games are no longer played but instead the picturehouse claims their attention and who shall say for the better?

The old custom of ceilidhing still survived and helped to pass the winter nights. Stories were told and riddles solved, a singsong and impromptu dance, if a musician of any sort was there; if not a lilter took his place. The stories have come down through the generations and were much of the same colour. It might have been a winding sheet that hovered over a house before a death there; or it might have been some troubled soul that left a debt unpaid and wanted some friend to do the needful; or it could have been a coach and four that used to gallop past a certain place at a furious speed, and though could not be seen, was supposed to be a one-time tyrannical landlord, still carrying on but with a different coachman! Of course, the big dog with rattling chains and blazing eyes at some lonely spot was always to the fore; and the fellow who met the countryman coming from a card school on a summer morning and persuaded him to set down by the road fence and have a few more games. The stranger was winning ahead, when the countryman chanced to look down, noticed the cloven foot and, making an excuse, said he would have to be going! The ghost stories cleared the house well before twelve o'clock, as only after that hour were they abroad. The Banshee was not a ghost. She was a harmless little lady, dressed in white who keened weirdly on the death

of members of certain families, who claimed it was proof of
their ancient line and prided in the reputation of the Banshee's
wailing when death came to the household. Of course, all the
stories were not hair raising: the Leprechaun with his money
bags, the fairy dances by moonlight and many others that
brought laughter and jokes.

Those harmless enjoyable ceilidhe meetings were casual
without any previous arrangement and it depended on the
number of people dropping into a house whether the session
would be long or short, if at all. Never again can the ceilidhes
as of old be revived. The folklore of Éire must remain a story
of the past. The cinema and radio have settled that for good.
Seventy years ago, not only had misrule decimated the race
but had reduced what remained of it to a condition of ignorance and servitude rendering the people absolutely helpless.
They had no voice in political affairs nor in the administration
of the law. A poor law guardianship was about the highest
position they might aspire to and, even there, the Ascendancy
ruled by votes or influence. Previous to the enactment of the
Ballot Act in 1872, voting at elections was an open affair and
anybody who wished could know how another voted. A £10
property valuation was a necessary qualification for a voter.
Parliamentary candidates were chiefly of the upper or
Ascendancy class but for parliamentary honours there was a
good deal of jealousy and elections were hotly contested.
Even though not candidates themselves, landlords took sides,
and saw that their tenants voted as they wished. Bribery,
intimidation and free drinks were all employed to influence
the result. Farmers and their sons could be seen marching in
a body, armed with bludgeons, to the polling station to make
sure that there would be no interference with the supporters of
their landlord or his nominee, and he or his agent would be
present to see that his tenants voted as he desired. A tenant
who had the temerity to vote against his landlord might expect
eviction proceedings in due course. There was no freedom
whatever in connection with those elections. But it mattered
little to the people, as Ireland concerned the British House of

Commons only to the extent of being a useful appendage and making sure that the Queen's writ ran there.

In 1872, the Ballot Act brought a mighty change. At the time it could be regarded as a charter of liberty. It was the first effective blow landlordism had received. The return of some sixty Home Rulers at the general election of 1874 was ample evidence of the change; under the open system of voting it is questionable if one Home Ruler would have been elected. It may be imagined the condition of slavery the people had reached when found marching in a body to vote and cheer and fight for their age long oppressors! But as we have seen the people had to live and however degrading their lot set themselves to the task; they had settled down to live within the law as no other course was open to them. The country was peaceable, with the exception of the usual spasmodic outbreaks in the North and faction fights in the South, but these did not affect the general peace. The cultivation of the land was the great and, in most instances, the only means left the people for existence. While there was, say, twenty-five per cent of the people—large farmers, shopkeepers, and others—in comfortable circumstances, the great majority toiled for a living. Their homes were poor and little regard was paid to sanitation. They were absolutely ignorant of such matters and could not see the dangers that existed in and around their homes. Periodic outbreaks of infectious diseases were frequent, especially among the very poor. In every assembly of the people, men and women could be seen bearing on their faces the marks of an attack of small pox which they had providentially survived. Little or no State attention was given to the health of the people. Members of the family attended those who were sick as best they could. There were dispensary doctors but the people did not trouble them nor did they trouble about the people. There were no nurses outside the hospitals. People sickened and died in their homes without any help, except what they received from their neighbours; they had an aversion to entering hospitals, especially a county hospital, because it was an appendix to the workhouse, and savoured of pauperism.

Left to their own resources, people sought remedies for illness in herbs and plants, and roots, and believed in their efficacy. The experience of grandfathers and grandmothers was always at hand to advise in the use of them. Some individuals were regarded as having exceptional skill—"quack doctors"—and many of them were preferred to some doctors. Some of them specialised in setting broken limbs and were called "bone setters". Quack doctors charged fees for their services. Others claimed to have charms for curing certain diseases. This was a sort of occult power, claimed to have come down in certain families for the cure of particular diseases. Certain herbs known only to the operator were, with other ingredients, mystically concocted and, as a plaster, applied outwardly or, if in liquid form, drunk to effect a cure. The gift of curing styes, by pointing gooseberry thorns at them with prayers, belonged to the seventh son of parents of the same surname before marriage. The amusing, if mean, method of transferring warts from one to another required no occult gift. The infected person rubbed the warts with a rag, which was then made up in a neat packet to look like something worth picking up and left in the way of passers by. The person picking up the packet took over the warts in a short time from the other one.

Superstition entered a good deal into the lives of the people; but every country had its superstitions. Many of the superstitions were amusing. Some people, especially women, were believed to have an "evil eye" and had the power of taking milk from the cows, and the butter from the milk—meaning that the owners of the cows failed to get milk from them, or that no butter would come from the milk when churned. The person of the evil eye, although having no cows, had plenty of milk and butter! Then there was the red haired woman, whom it was always unlucky to meet first in the morning. People going to a fair with cattle and meeting, first on the road, a red haired woman, said they might as well turn back, as they would not have any luck that day. Luck was, and is, greatly mixed up with cattle—hence the "luck penny". The magpie was an omen of luck and coming events; one seen alone boded ill luck, two together a marriage, and three a christening. Many other instances could be given as an example of the innocence and credulity of the people. In their innocence they were probably more content than if they knew more: their ambitions were few, and their disappointments less.

The old custom of waking the dead for two nights before burial was continued until the priests a few years ago caused the corpse to be removed to the parish church until the day of interment. Originally, the wake was probably a religious vigil but in time became more or less a friendly, sympathetic gathering; indeed not always with due respect for the dead, especially by the youth that assembled there. Still, notwithstanding objectionable levity that crept into the custom, it remained a token of sympathy and respect. Neighbouring people assembled at the house of death in the evening and remained one or two hours until others arrived and so on during the night. Seating accommodation was provided and clay pipes filled with tobacco were served to all comers. They smoked and chatted in groups but amusing stories and hilarity were often a feature, not in keeping with the solemnity to be expected on such an occasion. This led to the clergy intervening and ruling that the corpse should be removed to the church until the date of burial, after due religious ceremonial. The change was very proper and satisfactory, as it meant a saving of trouble and expense to the bereaved family and did not prevent people calling and tendering sympathy. A very nice old custom used to exist in country districts on the occasion of a death. Immediately, neighbouring people used to cease unnecessary work until after the funeral of the deceased. The old custom of keening at wakes and funerals was just passing away in the earliest recollections of the writer. Only on two occasions did he hear that wailing lamentation by women trained to give expression to it. These old customs were but the outcome of all that was best in the Irish character—heartfelt sympathy springing from a generous nature for anyone meeting trouble.

I was about to close this chapter when it occurred to me whether I should not say something about a class that has almost vanished. This was the tramping fraternity. These were men who would not work, even if offered it. They lived by tramping the roads all over. They kept to the road all the time, begging on the way, where there seemed a chance of getting food or money. A workhouse was their chief resting place and, if one was not within reach, they put up in cheap lodgings or turned into a hay shed or, in fine weather, took up a sheltered position on the other side of the road fence. The workhouse was much more in their line, for there they got bed and breakfast free but were compelled to do some work before being discharged; this was breaking stones or something they did not relish. From workhouse to workhouse they kept going, picking up what they could on the way and helping one another if possible when they met. Those who had a voice or a musical instrument—even a tin whistle—sang and played in the towns and were able to get along without calling at the workhouse. The patron of the workhouse was the typical "weary Willie". Many of them were harmless, but not all. A policeman was told off to visit the low lodging houses at night and the workhouse in the morning to interview them, as some of them might have been wanted. They were a worthless, unpopular lot; nobody wanted them. But there they were, a feature of life in the country and so I am jotting them down.

Another class of tramp was the itinerant tradesman. He was not the "weary Willie" type. As a rule, he was a good tradesman but never settled for long in one place. He tramped from town to town until he got a job. If he failed to get a job, his fellow craftsmen subscribed sufficient to help him to the next town and so he continued until he "struck oil". Then he settled down and seemed quite content, meeting his fellows on Saturday nights, having a social drink and apparently quite at home. Three or four months, or perhaps less, passed and he and his employers were getting along without complaint. A day came, however, when he did not turn up to work. He had been seen in more than one public house during the day. Next morning he called on the boss, told him he was leaving and requested whatever money was due to him. It was useless for his employer to try to persuade him to stay. The "call of the road" had reached him; it was in his blood and he could tarry no longer. A few drinks, and away he went, probably with another on the move. They were not obliged to inquire the turn to take when they reached a crossroads. They had the geography of the country on the tips of their fingers—the distance to the "Cat and Bagpipes", "Hare and Hounds", "Fighting Cocks", or other public house on their itinerary, they could tell to the perch, and the name of the owner in most instances. So they lived their lives, never settling in any place. They had no family responsibility and their spare cash went in drink. Old age came in time and they usually wound up in a pauper's grave.

Another institution, which has deteriorated beyond recognition in its present representatives, was the tinsmith trade, which machinery and advanced ideas have pushed aside. In the period covered by this book, bands of tinkers moved through the country, each having a roughly defined trading area established by custom, which was recognised and respected by the others. Their trade, I need not say, was an exclusive one, and they made good money—*except occasionally*—ate and drank well, and clothed comfortably. They were big, powerful men and women and, as they lived constantly in the open, were weatherproof. They paid neither rent nor rates, living in roughly constructed shelters in bye roads and waste corners, where they plied their trade, their women hawking their output in the surrounding district. Except when they drank more than was good for them—and that was pretty often—they gave little trouble. They were careful not to give cause for complaint that might land in their being shifted by the police. They remained in one place only as long as business was good, unless for some cause the police compelled them to move. When on the move, it sometimes happened that they made contact with another band changing their quarters. As there were intermarriages among them all, the meeting was usually a cordial one. If the meeting took place in or near a town, they proceeded to celebrate the occasion. From one public house to another, they drank and feasted, men and women, a happy family. Notwithstanding kinship, there were generally old sores in the background and, when the drink began to stir their blood, some outstanding question, charged with trouble, came under discussion. A few hot words and blackthorn sticks and perhaps soldering irons came into action, and soon men were sprawling on the ground with bloody heads, and women too, with hair dishevelled and faces damaged. The affair was short and sharp and when the police arrived their action depended on the condition of the party from drink and wounds. Of course there would be Court proceedings but, if the wounds were not serious, that did not trouble the rioters; they were often there before.

Socially, those rough, crude bands of men and women were regarded as outside the constitution and people felt uncomfortable in the neighbourhood where they encamped. Still, there they had been for generations—a necessary evil if you like—each band maintaining its patrimony, notwithstanding intermarriages, and was known as "The McDonoughs", "The Joyces", "The Cartys", etc. Although they had bloody rows when drink was going, they forgot them and fraternised at their next meeting, as though nothing had happened. In time of trouble, they had no friends outside their own circle and then it must be said they were loyal to one another. After all, those people were born into and grew up in that condition of life and never had a chance of being anything but what they were. Let us not then be too hard on their memory. Perhaps with all their faults, people will be found to say "they had their good points"; but the writer could hardly assent.

Let us pass from the vagrant units to a more reputable class, which were always welcome visitors. These were the respectable travelling musicians, who used to delight the inhabitants of the various towns with beautiful music, rendered in excellent style. They were well-conducted people who earned a decent living by their profession and were the joy of the town while they remained. Sometimes two or three would perform together. The violinists and pipers were the most popular, as they excelled in Irish music, especially dance music. Crowds used to follow them through the streets in the evenings, and doors and windows used to be full of the inmates. That source of pleasure for townspeople has vanished and in its place we have the cinema; yet, those old street musicians would, I believe, still have a surpassing charm for the people.

Let us not forget the German bands which, too, were always welcome. What beautiful music, instrumentally and vocally, they used to give out. The Great War of 1914–18 called them all to the fatherland and they have never since returned. Many people said they were military officers surveying the country; and who can tell? Nor can we say that a time will come when a German officer, leading an invading column of soldiers, may one day be seen consulting a map prepared by a member of one of those very bands which used to contribute so much to the enjoyment of the people.

One other traveller I think is worthy of notice. He was an American, named Doc Sequah. He travelled from town to town in a two-horsed wagon with a band, delivering discourses publicly from the wagon on various ailments which he professed to be able to cure. Herbs, which he had discovered on American prairies, were the secret of his success. In the evenings, after serenading the town with his wagon and band, he took up a position in public and gave demonstrations of his ability to give relief to sufferers. Men crippled by rheumatism were invited to get up on the wagon for treatment, free of cost. He took but one or two of an evening and massaged the affected parts in a screened part of the wagon with an embrocation he had compounded from the prairie flowers. The patient was then told to get off the wagon and test the result. Usually it was an apparent success, for the subject could walk with a freedom of action that surprised himself. Again, he professed to be able to extract teeth without causing pain. Sufferers took a seat on the wagon and Sequah set to work. During the operation, the band struck up a rousing tune and drowned the groans and bawls of the man in the chair. Holding up the forceps, with the villainous tooth held firmly, Sequah triumphantly faced the crowd, and the crowd cheered. "Seeing is believing", and thus Sequah advertised his skill and, it was said, made a fortune. He put up in first class hotels, where he prescribed privately for sufferers, charging a guinea for the first interview. He visited every city and town of any note in the country and eventually returned to America. A short time ago, I saw an account of his death. He must have reached a ripe old age—around 90 I would say. With his band he made a noise in every town. His evening discourses and public treatment of rheumatism and offending teeth were a source of merriment to the crowds that surrounded his wagon. He was very popular. Children in every town fifty years ago could be heard in bunches singing—"Doctor Sequah came to town, riding on a pony, he rubbed them up and rubbed them down, and left them all aloney" (meaning they could then walk without help)!

These are some of the features of life in the generation now passing fast away and may help many of the present generation to see the change that has taken place in a lifetime. That is my object in jotting them down in simple terms so that it may contribute to a clearer view of life in the country, of the period covered by these pages.

CHAPTER SEVENTEEN.

THE PARNELL COMMISSION.

Many episodes in the history of the Force could be quoted showing the unscrupulous employment of men to carry out the policy of the Government; but in connection with the Parnell Commission of Inquiry into the Pigott forgeries, alleging sympathy with and approval of the Phoenix Park murders and other crimes by the Irish Parliamentary Party, the attitude of the Government was the most striking. Although a matter of great public importance, it was a question between Parnell and the "London *Times*" and one would think should have been left to the *Times* people to prove their case. Instead, the Government employed the R.I.C. to ransack every police office in the country for records of "outrages" following speeches at public meetings, and many other matters that would go to imply complicity by the Parliamentary Party. Men from every district, having knowledge of such occurrences, were brought to London to be examined as witnesses before the Commission and were maintained in first class hotels until the collapse of the case. When Mr Arthur Balfour, then Chief Secretary, was questioned in the House of Commons on the employment of the police in such a way, he answered that he would keep the ring between the parties and that if the Irish Party desired access to police records he would let them have it. It was a good holiday for the police. Out of dishfuls of gold they were paid liberal expenses; a bit of luck that seldom came their way.

The assassination of Lord Frederick Cavendish and Mr Burke on that Saturday evening, 6 May 1882, was the greatest blow to Parnell and the Irish cause that could be inflicted at the time. It was a cowardly, brutal assassination, the savagery of which could scarcely be paralleled. The people stood aghast at the enormity of the crime—so foreign to their instincts—which could only bring shame on the country. Lord Frederick Cavendish had come on a friendly mission and there was nothing to show that Mr Burke was inimical to the Irish people. He was a subordinate in the Chief Secretary's office, carrying out the views of his chief and was not responsible for the policy of the Government. At the time, as a young Constable, I had access to official correspondence and, in Mr. Burke's minutes, there was always noticeable a sympathetic spirit. In matters of evictions and otherwise, his observations were not on the side of harshness but often contained sympathetic suggestions, more than was customary with Castle officials. He usually wrote with red ink in a small neat hand, enclosing his initials T.H.B. with a circular sweep of the pen. I have seen it stated that he was one of the Castle anti-Irishmen deserving of his fate. This assertion has been made without a scrap of evidence so far as the public is aware and in all probability without any foundation. In official circles the Park tragedy created consternation. The police were in motion all over the country. Every stranger wearing a sou'wester hat was accosted and questioned, as the description of the murderers circulated set out that hats of that pattern were worn by them. This was information probably supplied by some person who had not seen them at all. It was thought at the time that, after committing the crime, they were more likely to have made for the country than the city. At all events, as is now known, the police were at sea for long and hope of their success seemed to have vanished when Superintendent Mallon and his assistants received information that led to the arrest and conviction of the murderers.

CHAPTER EIGHTEEN.

EMIGRATION.

In the terrible years of famine and resultant disease in the late 1840s, it is calculated that one and a half million of the population perished. History tells that in the early 1850s the people were bewildered and dumbfounded, unable to see what to do or where to run, so hopeless was their outlook. Small landholders, who made up the majority of those on the land, were unable to pay rent or rates and were evicted wholesale to go where they might and live or die. Some were allowed to settle on waste lands and mountain slopes where, even today, may be seen recorded in some instances the grass-grown outlines of the last ridges of potatoes, before giving up the hopeless task of living there and moving, God knows where! Those who could make their way to other countries, especially to America, did so in thousands and those thousands, in time, brought other thousands; so that the flight from the country increased to such an extent that the English Press, led by the London *Times*, shouted out exultantly that the Celt was gone or going and that soon an Irishman would be as rare as a Red Indian on the shores of Manhattan. The Irish are here yet and little did England think, in her brutal might that, in her effort to destroy the race, she was engaged in creating a force that, with bitter memories, would one day stand in her path to be reckoned with.

Down through the 1860s and 1870s, the stream of emigration still flowed, draining the country of its manhood and womanhood. The old sailing vessels were still employed, at least in the 1860s, to carry passengers. The voyage to America took about four weeks. The passengers supplied themselves with food. I remember intending emigrants preparing for the voyage packing boxes of food, the principal item being large oatmeal cakes baked hard in front of a bright turf fire, supported by a metal stand or two sods of turf. The cake was circular, about eight or nine inches in diameter, and about a quarter of an inch thick. Baked hard, it would remain good for months and was a most sustaining food. I doubt if many women could now be found to produce one of those wonderful cakes, once seen in most Irish homes. They were capable of being broken into convenient pieces without waste and people on a long fatiguing journey usually brought a supply with them.

The night before leaving, neighbours and friends assembled in the house of the party about to emigrate to give them a "send off". With tea, a bottle of whiskey perhaps, which was cheap at the time, a "sing-song" and dance, the night was passed. The songs were chiefly of a sentimental strain, lamenting having to leave "dear old Ireland" but promising to return when landlords had met their doom and a brighter sun would shine. But alas, few who left in those days ever returned! Some never reached their destination, being lost on their way. Whole families, helped by their friends in America, used to go. One family, I remember, was believed to have been lost when no account of the arrival of the ship had been received within a reasonable time. Ultimately, however, news came that it had been wrecked on Prince Edward Island, but that the passengers had been saved and eventually had reached the friendly shores of Columbia.

To return to the sends-off: morning came and saw the emigrant on the way, convoyed to the railway station if convenient, or part of the way, if at a distance. If in later times, when America had become so near and the voyage without risk, we have witnessed distressful scenes when members of families left to join their friends there, what must have been the heart rendings when parents and children were parting with little hope of ever again meeting on earth. Brave hearts were needed to face the perils of an Atlantic voyage in those old sailing vessels, rightly described as "coffin ships". Terrible tales were told of passengers being hatched down in suffocating conditions in periods of storm. It is on record that in one instance one of those old hulks put into Derry and dumped on the quay fifty or sixty bodies of people who had been suffocated while hatched down. Little care was taken to keep those old vessels in a sanitary condition and passengers often contracted diseases in them during the voyage. I remember one fine young man of whom the first news received after landing was an account of his death from yellow fever, believed to have been picked up on the ship.

I used to hear of the unbounded joy of the passengers when it was announced that "land was in sight". At once there was joyful bustle and excitement. All set to wash and dress and get ready to set foot at last on the land of their dreams and hopes after their long and trying voyage. What courage and what nobility of soul actuated those inexperienced boys and girls to face such a perilous ordeal, so that they might succour the dear ones they had left behind, must be left to the imagination. Long, long ago, away back in the early 1860s, I remember being in a mud cabin, where a young woman sat driving a shuttle on a handloom. Her younger sister came in with a small jug in her hand. Resting on the loom and looking at her sister, the young woman said sadly but deter-minedly "I hope to see the day Mary, when you won't have to ask the neighbours for a sup of milk for our tea". That young woman got to America and, in a remarkably short time, brought the entire family of five: and the ship in which they sailed was the one wrecked on Prince Edward Island.

Nowadays, we hear a good deal about the flight from the land, when the people themselves own the land and, in the greater portion of the country, are freemen. In days gone by, it was the dearest wish of the people to remain on the land, even under tyrannical conditions. What a heaven-sent boon it would have been for the past generation to have been placed as are the people of today!

Nor did the Irish exiles forget. In the land of their adoption those sons and daughters of Ireland remained true to their motherland; time only increased their love of country and friends. One can visualise those boys and girls, wherever fate had cast their lives, whether in city, plain or woodland, ever looking back to the old land and recalling the scenes of their youth—the old roads and lanes, hills and dells, their associations and all the recollections of their young lives, making up a picture that neither time nor conditions would dim—a picture lovingly dwelt upon while life remained. Love of country, inherent in the human breast, is a distinctive trait of the Irish character, notable especially when seas intervene; even an Orangeman, who in Ireland may be said to be a man without a country, is a good Irishman in a strange land and will shake hands with and find fellowship in a Fenian! It is remarkable that if an Irishman or women is indifferent towards their country they are found, as a rule, degenerate in other respects as well. Love of Irish exiles for their sea-girt homeland has not been confined to her scenic charms, her virtues, and her homeliness but has been manifest beyond calculation in the constant support given to their kith and kin in their long struggle to regain the freedom of their country. Who shall assess the millions of money remitted across the seas, not only from America but from every land where found, by the faithful sons and daughters of Ireland and their descendants to sustain their people against landlord tyranny and English rule, so long the bane of their country. Even yet, the American letter, especially the Christmas one, comes along to bring comfort and cheer to thousands of homes.

Cobh (Queenstown) was the chief port of embarkation for Munster and midland counties and must have seen many thousands of emigrants on the way to America. Cobh is built on the side of a hill, sloping down to the water's edge. Overlooking the town is the beautiful cathedral, towards the erection of which the American Irish were generous contributors. The site of that magnificent structure would seem to have been specially selected for the benefit of emigrants. Standing well up on the hillside overlooking the harbour, its graceful spire, topped by a large glinting cross, must be visible far out to sea. One can conceive the majestic symbol making a last impression on Catholic emigrants crowding the decks as the ship sailed out and flashing, as it were, farewell signals and admonishing them, through weal and woe, ever to hold dear the faith of their fathers; nor is it likely that last view of Cobh was ever effaced from the memory of the thousands of Irish youth who sailed out from its waters!

CHAPTER NINETEEN.

GAIN VERSUS ODDS.

Let us now glance at the changes which have taken place within the lifetime of many who are still with us.

English rule is no longer known in twenty-six of the thirty-two counties; landlordism has disappeared from the entire country; in the twenty-six counties the people are absolutely independent, acknowledging no outside authority; the people have the making and unmaking of their own laws; they have their own Constitution, setting out the fundamental laws under which they desire to live; they have their own judges to interpret and dispense their laws; their own police to see that the laws are obeyed; their own civil servants, manning the various civil departments of the State; their own army to defend the State; and, over all, their own Parliament, elected by themselves and answerable to them for their stewardship. The independence of the State is recognised by all civilised governments, the principal of which have their ministers representing their interests in the seat of government. The national flag, the emblem of nationhood, has supplanted the union jack on the ramparts of Dublin Castle, which holds so many bitter memories for the race. And now let us see the odds against which this freedom has been won.

Seventy years ago and later, Ireland was an amusing subject for the English people. The theatres and music halls had dished up to their audiences side-splitting presentations of the buffoonery of the Irish people. In the comic sheets, Paddy was padded with badly fitting breeches and a pipe in his hat and sometimes, as a variation, driving a pig. Pat and the pig were supposed to have much in common. But a time came when Pat and his friend attained a more reputable position. During the Great War, I remember seeing a princess of royal blood pictured in an English newspaper with a handsome young pig in her arms, as something of value. That was the time when both Pat and the pig were playing an important part in winning the Great War—that was the time when Pat was marching to the strains of "Tipperary" to man the trenches "for the freedom of small nations".

Let us return to the period when Gladstone realised that Ireland's national aspirations would have to be recognised and set himself the task of educating the English people of the need to appease what could not be killed by coercion. Then it was that the rich, powerful ruling classes of England, with vast interests, prejudiced to the core against the great majority of the Irish people, determined more than ever to stand in the way of any change towards a people so unfitted for self government, whose troubles were due to innate crassitude and indolence; that in fact they did not really know what they wanted. The Ascendancy party here was, of course, at all times up against any change that would whittle away "an inch" of their preserves. To hand the Freemasons over to disloyalty was something that could not happen, and would not happen, and in secret conclave with their brothers in Dublin Castle they kept devising plans to thwart such an evil. On top of all was the English Press availing themselves of every opportunity to defame the Irish people in the eyes of the world and to poison the minds of the English people towards this country.

All this the great English statesman had to contend with when he set out to give Ireland a native government. During the last decade of his great liberal career, he devoted his matchless ability and eloquence to Ireland's cause. Through the defection of a section of his party, led by Mr. Joseph Chamberlain, he failed in 1886 to carry a Home Rule measure, resulting in the fall of his administration. Again in power in 1893, with marvellous energy and eloquence at the age of 84 he overcame all opposition and passed through the House of Commons a Home Rule Bill which, though only of limited scope, was promptly thrown out by the House of Lords. Though the great statesman failed in what he hoped would be the crowning achievement of his historic career, he chalked up a headline that remained.

Later on we saw Sir Edward (afterwards Lord) Carson and his aide-de-camp "Galloper Smith" (afterwards Lord Birkenhead) preaching sedition and instigating mutiny in military circles, because another government was about to propose another Home Rule measure; and we saw those treason mongers, instead of being put on trial as criminals, raised, one to the House of Lords, the other to the Lord Chancellorship of England, and the mutinous Curragh officers continued in the service without censure.

It took the armed conflicts of 1916 and 1920 at last to bring home to England the need for change towards this country, but this is history outside the limits of this book.

In Gladstone's Home Rule measure there was no approach to the independence such as the country now enjoys; nor did the country hope for such. Does this generation realise what has been won for the twenty-six counties and, let us hope, soon for the other six—against opposition regarded by the past generation as insurmountable in their time? Do the young men and young women of Ireland realise the heritage that has come their way? They have a country with all its natural resources undeveloped and in a most favourable position for intercourse and trade with other countries, and it is up to them to make the most of the chance they have got, to make Éire one of the happiest lands. But this will not be accomplished by a wave of the wand; it will take time and perseverance. To bring about that happy state of affairs there must be united endeavour. Without unity little or no headway can be made and no less essential is an honest rendering of one's best in whatever may be his or her avocation. As an incentive to fulfilling wholeheartedly the trust which has been handed down to this generation, the best is to read Irish history.

CHAPTER TWENTY.

A FEW WORDS MORE.

In these pages, I desire to state that I have not been influenced by any consideration other than to set out truly my experience in the police and the conditions of life in the country. The Royal Irish Constabulary has been misrepresented, not only in Ireland but also in other countries and it is only right that a just appreciation of that Force should go down in the history of its time. No doubt, the Whelehan and Sheridan episodes contributed largely to the misleading conception that the R.I.C. was a reprehensible institution. I remember reading a reference to it by a French newspaper which described it as "an infamous police". My chief purpose, then, has been to correct that erroneous estimate of a Force which as a body was unequalled in point of rectitude by any other police force in the world.

In matters bearing on the history of Ireland, religion cannot be passed over if the truth is to be told and, if I have been obliged to show how it entered into the lives of the police and people, I have not been actuated by either bigotry or malice. I have always held that religion is a person's own private affair and to question the freedom of its exercise, without cause, is a rude impertinence; but to penalise unjustifiably a person because of his religion is nothing short of a gross outrage on his rights. Some time ago, I was pleased to read in the report of a speech by a Belfast Protestant gentleman an expression of similar views. It is to be hoped that gentleman's conception of tolerance is spreading in the six counties and that the time is not far distant when the people of that area will be found in step with the rest of their fellow countrymen for the good of all.

ADDENDUM.

The record of my experience in the R.I.C. was compiled
some years ago but its publication has been delayed chiefly
because of the [Second World] War. Since then I have read
Miss McArdle's book *The Irish Republic*, Piaras Beaslai's *Michael
Collins and the Making of a New Ireland* and *The American and
English Labour Commissions' Reports of their findings on the conditions
of Ireland during 1920–21*. These are the most noteworthy publications that have yet appeared on the Anglo-Irish Conflict;
yet though I have found a good deal of interest in the reading
of them I would not in consequence change a line I had
written in my booklet; and anything I have to say in relation
to them, I consider better as an Addendum than to confuse
my simple narrative with a discussion of outsiders whose
knowledge of the R.I.C. was, at best, only superficial.

All those authorities have as a matter of course a good deal
to say about the R.I.C., very much of which is entirely
misleading. Miss McArdle alleges that they were a force of
spies and that the allegation was, according to her account,
even more vehemently urged by Mr de Valera on the occasion of his election as President of Dáil Éireann. Although
Mr Beaslai in the opening pages of his book refers to the
R.I.C. as a Force whose chief employment was espionage, he
takes the sting out of the hurtful assertion in the course of his
comprehensive work.

At all times there were people ever ready to charge the
R.I.C. as spies and pliant tools of the English Government

and now, more than ever, this was the allegation advanced to justify the wanton attack made upon them; Miss McArdle goes as far almost to say that they were inborn spies when she asserts that, before admission into the Force, every candidate was obliged to attend at Dublin Castle. She does not say for what purpose but the inference is that it was something in the nature of a blood test. Now the fact is that not one in a hundred ever entered the Castle at any time or scarcely knew its situation in the City. "No body of men", she states, "ever served their paymasters with more loyalty than the Royal Irish Constabulary". That is an entire misconception: the R.I.C. were anything but loyal to the English Government. They were loyal to themselves and those depending on them. Could loyalty be expected of men living under circumscribed crushing conditions? If they were obliged to be active in carrying out the work imposed upon them it did not mean loyalty; instead it went far to engender disloyalty. Miss McArdle is nearer the mark when she states "That loyalty was always in conflict with their own natural feelings".

The loyalty of the Royal Irish Constabulary was put to the test on two notable occasions. During the Boer War and the European War of 1914–18, the R.I.C. were appealed to for Volunteers with very disappointing results. About a dozen volunteered for Africa and not more than fifty went to France.[1] No: the R.I.C. were no more loyal than the majority of their fellow countrymen nor even as loyal in many instances, when it is remembered that the brunt of the fighting in the Great War was borne by hundred of thousands of Irishmen, most of whom were volunteers influenced, however it is but fair to state, by the perfidious delusion that they were fighting for the freedom of small nations, especially that of their own.

---

1   This very low figure contradicts the more plausible figure of 752 officers and men cited in J. Herlihy, *The Royal Irish Constabulary: A Short History and Genealogical Guide* (Dublin: Four Courts Press, 1977)

The work of supplying the Government with all sorts of information has been advanced as proof of the system of espionage. In the body of my book I have described that system. Posted in small parties all over the country, the R.I.C. in common with the people had knowledge of all public matters, political and otherwise, and the attitude of the people towards them. There were no conspiracies or secrets to be unearthed and the police were able to supply the Government with any information required without engaging in espionage. If unable of their own knowledge to do so, they had little difficulty in obtaining it without recourse to deceitful methods. All this work devolved on Sergeants in charge of Stations and District Inspectors and was a source of worry instead of a labour of love. It did not concern the rank and file to the extent of a decimal point. Much of all this work was the outcome of Castle Officialism and was of little value beyond throwing dust in the eyes of the English people and even of Chief Secretaries.

If at any time the R.I.C. had no reason to be loyal to the English Government they had very much less during 1920–1, though Miss McArdle would have her readers believe that their mentality was such that the infamous "Weekly Summary" hissing out serpent-like from behind the ramparts of Dublin Castle hatred of the bravest of the race, had incited the police, as well as the military and Black and Tans, to commit cowardly murders; and as proof she cites the murder of a hunchback at Bantry, where all the evidence showed that this cruel murder was committed by the Black and Tans. But this is only one instance that, without discrimination, Miss McArdle would seem to convey that the R.I.C. were hand-in-glove with the Black and Tans in their unheard of cowardly crimes against the Irish people.

Miss McArdle also quotes from a book written by General Crozier, ten years afterwards, that on his arrival here as Commander of the Auxiliaries he found the R.I.C. demoralised and employed to murder, rob, loot and burn up the innocent, because they could not catch the few guilty on the run, but that he found the British Army in Ireland well behaved. What value Miss McArdle sees in this statement it is difficult to understand, either as to the demoralisation of the R.I.C. or the good conduct of the military. Regarding the police, it is an absolute falsehood and, as to the conduct of the military, her own book in various instances shows that it was the military and not the police that were demoralised. She reproduces an article by Erskine Childers in the *Daily News*, describing a typical night in Dublin of raiding by the military and also an account by an ex-officer of an excursion by lorry to Balla, County Mayo of a party of Argyle Highlanders where, after getting drunk in a public house, the owner sought the assistance of the local R.I.C. who persuaded them to leave for their station, Claremorris. The lorry stopped at a gypsy encampment outside the town and one of the men tried to enter a tent in which a woman was sleeping and, when prevented, fired his rifle point blank into the tent, dangerously wounding the old woman. That night at 11 p.m. these soldiers returned to the town, fired into the police barracks, proceeded to shoot up the town, entered public houses, firing shots through the ceilings, and demanded more drink. Then they broke into the Convent grounds, entered the Keeper's Lodge, asked him if he had any daughters and burst into a bedroom where three young girls of sixteen to twenty years were in bed. One of the soldiers loaded his rifle, pointed it at the youngest, threatening to shoot her if she did not keep quiet. Another tried to disarm him and during the struggle the girls escaped in their nightdresses to the Convent for protection.

In the House of Commons on 22 June, Denis Henry, Attorney General for Ireland, stated that the British troops in Ireland had been instructed to behave as if on a battlefield; but their battlegrounds were in the homes of the Irish people and their behaviour was not that of disciplined soldiers waging war. These are the men that General Cozier found well behaved.

After describing the mutiny of the police in Kerry, which she takes from the *Irish Bulletin*, Miss McArdle states that "elsewhere the police were more amenable to their instructions", and she quotes instances of alleged destruction by them in Bantry, Limerick, Newcastle West, and other places, without a particle of evidence that they had done so in compliance with instructions or, in fact, that they had done so at all. But Miss McArdle's charges against the R.I.C. as I have shown in other instances are not to be taken without question.

Lloyd George knew that the R.I.C. would not engage in murder and arson, and so he dressed the Black and Tans and Auxiliaries in R.I.C. uniform and called them police, in order to camouflage their crimes as mere frolics measured for the protection of the law-abiding. Even the American Commission and the English Labour Commission it would seem were unable to see clearly the distinction between the R.I.C. and the Black and Tans and Auxiliaries.

Now reverting to the charge of espionage, as I have shown the R.I.C. were able to supply the Government with all sorts of information without recourse to espionage. There was no need for it; and if there had been, the R.I.C. would have been the most useless agency for such a purpose. Cunning and deceit are most essential qualifications of a spy but the R.I.C. were never schooled in these arts nor ever sailed under false colours. Indeed, one of their greatest faults was their attitude of independence from the people, from whom they were not obliged to look for favours; and, similarly, the people did not look to them for favours: the line was distinctly drawn. But that did not prevent friendly intercourse with the orderly well-behaved community.

Both Miss McArdle and Piaras Beaslai, in support of the charge of espionage, refer to the evidence of Mr Birrell before the Royal Commission into the 1916 Insurrection. As quoted by Mr. Beaslai, Mr. Birrell stated to the Commission "so far as the country generally is concerned, we had the reports of the Royal Irish Constabulary, who send us in reports almost daily from every district in Ireland, and I have them under the microscope. Their reports undoubtedly do enable anybody sitting in Dublin or London to form a correct general estimate of the feeling of the countryside in different localities". Now, the R.I.C. had eyes and ears as well as everybody else, and were able, if required, to supply information as to the attitude of the people towards matters engaging the public mind without recourse to espionage. Of their inefficiency as spies, no better example could be given than the 1916 Rising. Here was a revolutionary movement in existence throughout the country for a considerable period and of which the R.I.C. had less knowledge than the general public and when the outbreak took place no one was more surprised than the Chief Secretary himself.

There may have been and probably were in the ranks of the R.I.C. individuals who gave Auxiliaries and Black and Tans information of the names and addresses of Sinn Féiners and Republicans, but the great body of the men who shrank from association with those miscreants did not assist them in their campaign upon the people. It was not in the ranks of the R.I.C. the spies were to be found who gave information to the Auxiliaries and Black and Tans; nor were they all of the lower type of ex-army men and others, out for gain of one sort or another. In the supporters of English rule all over the country, the Crown Forces had ardent admirers who supplied them with information, when possible with safety, and some of these paid the usual penalty.

The R.I.C. did do some spying but it was not for the English cause. Piaras Beaslai, who was closely associated with Michael Collins throughout the conflict, tells us in his comprehensive chronicle of that eventful time that Michael Collins built up an organisation of friendly policemen within the R.I.C. and had men working for him in R.I.C. barracks in most of the important centres. These men were not allowed to resign and remained in the Force until the end of the war. Witnessing as they did the uncontrolled, infamous conduct of Lloyd George's bandits let loose on the people, the R.I.C. could not but feel resentment. When the chief agent of this outrage was no less a person than the Prime Minister of England, there remained no obligation on the R.I.C. to be faithful to such a regime; and when members played into the hands of the resourceful and audacious Michael Collins, they did a good day's work.

When we come to consider the attitude of the R.I.C. during the conflict it will be seen it was only when an armed attack was made upon them that, in self-defence, they had recourse to arms. It was in the early stages of the struggle that these attacks took place and the Force suffered most casualties. Lloyd George stated that between the end of the 1916 Rising and 10 July 1920, fifty-six police and four soldiers were killed.[2] While on patrol at night in twos and threes along country roads or moving about singly on any business through the streets of towns, unarmed, the R.I.C. could be shot down with little risk to the attackers; but to engage in attacks on the military was evidently regarded as a more dangerous operation. It was at this stage too that outlying stations, consisting of four or five men each, were attacked by armed parties. These attacks were made with the object of obtaining arms and ammunition. Not more than ten or twelve such attacks took place and only about half of these were successful. These were not fortified posts, as represented, but mere ordinary rented buildings in which the R.I.C. were housed all over the country. But one commendable feature in these assaults was that they were carried out in accordance with the usages of warfare. After surrendering and handing over their arms the defenders were set free. These were honourable operations and called for more—much more—valour than the ambushing of a couple of men from behind a stone fence. There were only a few casualties on either side in these attacks.

---

2   These figures are far too low—whether the fault is Lloyd George's or Fennell's is not clear. According to Herlihy, *The Royal Irish Constabulary*, the R.I.C. lost fourteen members killed due to political violence in 1916 and sixty-one members similarly 1919–end June 1920. For the latter period, the figure of fifty-eight killed is given by R. Abbott, *Police Casualties in Ireland 1919–1922* (Cork: Mercier Press, 2000). In fact, R.I.C. casualties were even higher in the subsequent eighteen months.

At first, there was little general control of the fighting elements of the revolution. Local parties acted chiefly on their own initiative and this to a great extent accounted for the indiscriminate shooting of the police. Law and order had ceased to exist and any crime could be committed with impunity. The people did not approve of the shooting of the R.I.C. but they stood dumbfounded and in terror and, no matter what they witnessed, remained silent. Nor did the real soldiers of the revolt, who were continually on the run, approve of the indiscriminate shooting of the police, in the ranks of which as well as among the retired members, they had plenty of friends. Those shootings as a rule were carried out by opportunists comparable only with camp followers killing the wounded in the wake of the firing line. Most of those attacks were much of a similar character. Patrolling the country roads by two men was one of the duties carried out at all times by the R.I.C. Having noticed a patrol going out and the road by which it was likely to return, an ambush by local parties was easily arranged. This would be at some suitable place previously selected and from which men could be shot down at close range without a chance of defending themselves. There was little heroism in those operations, or in shooting a man in the back on the streets of a town. Some of those murders were carried out with barbarous malignity.

The first of these was at Soloheadbeg, County Tipperary, on 21 January 1919, when two policemen were shot dead while escorting gelignite to a quarry for blasting purposes.[3] Police usually escorted explosives to see that care was taken to guard against accident to the public. As the horse and cart conveying the gelignite, with two men in charge, and the police escort of two Constables approached the quarry, something in the nature of a challenge by eight armed men in ambush astonished the car men and police, as they came along chatting

---

3 This incident is described by the leader of the IRA ambush party Dan Breen in his autobiography *My Fight for Irish Freedom* (Dublin: Anvil Books, 1981; first published by Talbot Press, 1924).

cheerily. They stopped, bewildered as to what it meant. Two shots from behind a gate pillar close by, and the two police-men fell dead! Briefly, this is what happened. As to the police making any attempt to use their arms, as alleged, no dispassionate reader of the published accounts of the ambush will believe that those men were not shot down before they got time to think or realise that they were in a death trap. They had no reason to fear any trouble for, once they saw the explosive safely delivered to the quarry official, their duty was finished and they would have returned to their station. Possession of the gelignite could then, or at some other time, have been got, doubtless with little trouble. The general con-demnation by the public as well as by the IRA Headquarters in Dublin of the crime shows what was thought of it at the time. The Coroner, who held the inquest, declared that the Constables "were nailed on the spot" and described the tragedy as one of the saddest that had occurred in County Tipperary or any other part of Ireland. He had known the Constables well, and that a more quiet, inoffensive man than Constable James McDonnell [R.I.C. 50616] who had been thirty years in Tipperary, he had never met, and that Constable Patrick O'Connell [R.I.C. 61889] was also a decent, quiet man. "It was sad to see these men shot down doing public duty, and not doing anything that would injure anybody". The son of Constable McDonnell rightly exclaimed that his father had not got "a dog's chance".

Again another shooting that shocked the people and filled their hearts with sorrow, that such an outrage could be charged to Catholic Ireland: at Bandon, when entering the chapel alone on Sunday morning for early Mass, a Sergeant was shot dead in the porch, when about to carry out the age long Catholic custom of sprinkling himself with holy water, before entering the sacred edifice.[4]

Every police force has an element of the people up against it—not entirely the criminal class—but those as well who do

4 Detective Sergeant William Mulherin (R.I.C. 61051), killed on 25 July 1920.

not want to be restricted in their actions by the laws of civilised society. These people are not actuated by politics or civic duties that run counter to their views and, of course, are at all times up against the police. Like every other agitation, the revolt was honeycombed by this class and those were the people, if they did nothing else, who joined industriously in the circulation of falsehoods against the police. It was even give out that it was the R.I.C. who murdered Father Griffin and, as a result, armed men entered a Galway nursing home and shot a Sergeant and a Constable who were in bed there under treatment. The Sergeant was shot dead but the Constable providentially recovered of his wounds but lost completely his eyesight. That the R.I.C. murdered Father Griffin was not generally believed; but General Crozier, who had command of the Auxiliaries, stated that he offered to give the name of the man who shot the priest, but no action was taken. Every falsehood of shooting people, espionage, and being the chief agents of English rule in the country was circulated to justify the wanton attack made on the Force. An attempt was even made to charge the R.I.C. with the burning of Cork but this was a complete failure.

Much of all this currency has been reproduced by Miss McArdle in her book but in scrappy generalities without a particle of evidence beyond that taken from propagandist sheets and other sources not stated. How unreliable were those reports at a time when it was unsafe for newspaper correspondents to be about in the neighbourhood of crimes committed by the Crown Forces, and perhaps days would elapse before news of these crimes would reach newspapers in anything but accurate shape?

The value that may be placed on Miss McArdle's generalities regarding the R.I.C. will be seen in two cold-blooded murders committed by military or Black and Tans and which she positively alleges were committed by the police. At page 409 of her book (3rd impression) she states: "On the day Kevin Barry was hanged Ellen Quinn was shot dead in Co. Galway by the police. She was sitting on her garden wall in Kiltartan with a child in her arms when they came tearing past in a lorry and fired. The only investigation made was a military inquiry at which the firing was found to be a precautionary measure."

Now, this tragedy attracted widespread attention at the time, not only because of its wantonness but of the fact that the victim was soon to give birth to another child. It was clearly established that the lorry was a military lorry containing military and that after passing Mrs. Quinn the fatal shot was fired from it. Evidence to the same effect was given before the American Commission which found—"In reference to Sir Hamar Greenwood's statement regarding the action of the military as indicating a moral tone regrettable in a public official of a civilised people, we would particularly emphasise his explanation of the death of Ellen Quinn, the expectant mother, who was shot wantonly by the military."

Again at page 434, Miss McArdle states that Mrs. Regan of Callan County Kilkenny was, on 23 December 1920, killed by the police. This was an instance exactly similar to the shooting of Mrs. Quinn. Mrs Ryan, not "Regan", was standing at her shop door when a lorry with Auxiliaries came racing through the town and after passing Mrs Ryan a shot was fired killing her.

In her general accusations against the R.I.C. Miss McArdle has recourse to Coroners' inquests as evidence of their guilt. Now a coroner's inquest is not a court of trial as to the guilt or otherwise of anyone concerned in the death of the subject of the inquiry. The chief function of a coroner's jury is to find the cause of death and anything outside this question is of no concern to the jury. The evidence as a rule is merely of a formal nature and is not regarded as proof or otherwise of the guilt of anyone accused of the death of the party. As to the value of these verdicts against the R.I.C. during the Troubles, here is an instance given by the English Labour Commission in their report: The Commission visited the village of Shanagolden where an attempt to burn the creamery was made by the Black and Tans. Next day the Local Volunteers arrested a Black and Tan and a policeman in connection with the occurrence and marched them up and down the street without their boots. As a reprisal, it is assumed, two lorries of Black and Tans arrived at the village in the evening and shot an old man of seventy-five years. *At the inquest a verdict of wilful murder was found against the police.*

This is another instance of how reflection has been cast on the R.I.C., by mixing them up with the Black and Tans without discrimination, and which confused the English and American Commissions. The difficulty of obtaining sufficient evidence rendered the finding of the American Commission not as complete or as accurate as it might have been by more informative testimony. No witness seems to have clearly informed the Commission as to the distinction between the R.I.C. and their Auxiliaries and the Black and Tans, else the Commission would not have arrived at this conclusion: "We have considered the evidence of eye-witnesses and depositions from victims, establishing that the 'Police' or 'Constabulary' includes in the ranks burglars and highway robbers, gunmen, and petty thieves. It was testified before us that the 'Police' or 'Royal Irish Constabulary' were charged by the British-appointed Coroner's Juries with the murders of Lord Mayor McCurtin and Messrs. Lynch, Walsh, Dwyer, McCarthy, Rooney and others. It was further testified that in other cases murders were committed by those so-called policemen and no jury was summoned. In the cases of Galway, Balbriggan and other cities and villages, these 'policemen' added arson and looting to murder. The presence of District Inspector Cruise at the reprisal in Galway and of District Inspector Lowndes at the sacking of Ballylorby, in charge of the sacking policemen, was mentioned in evidence. These persons have been corroborated in all essentials by the evidence of other witnesses, that the words 'police', 'Policemen' and 'constable', as used by the British in Ireland, are misleading and tend to reflect dishonour upon that class which in other lands maintain law and order."

Now in attributing to the R.I.C. the burning of Balbriggan, the Commission was under a complete misapprehension. This was the first act of incendiarism committed by the Auxiliaries after their arrival in March. A policeman was killed in the town.[5] As a reprisal two lorry loads of Auxiliaries, who were encamped a few miles away, arrived that evening and set fire to the hosiery factory and committed other acts of destruction to property. The bayoneting of two men on the street the following morning was committed by a soldier. The R.I.C. did not take any part in the acts except to try, as one Constable did, to stop further destruction.

As to the sacking of Ballylorby, it does not appear that anything more objectionable occurred than County Inspector Lowndes[6] and two young officers in charge of the military adjourned to a saloon and got drunk, and that the young officers set two terriers to fight outside the saloon door, and that some of the soldiers got drunk as well.

The evidence given by the resigned policemen seems coloured by exaggeration in some instances. Ex-Constable Caddan [R.I.C. 70263] who gave evidence of the alleged shooting up of Galway had been only a recruit of a few months' service and probably did not leave the barracks on the night in question.

The evidence of Father Cotter, an American priest on a visit to Galway, would go to show that it was a military party which did the shooting. Here is Father Cotter's evidence: "With the lights out and in my room I peeped out under the blinds and saw what appeared to be about 150 soldiers or police halt at the door of the hotel. Immediately after the order to halt came the word 'Fire'. So they shot there for several hours, terrifying everybody. I left my bed and lay under the window—it was a stone building—to escape a possible bullet." It is evident this was a party of military from the nearby barracks and the sacking and looting by the police while this was going on is very questionable.

5 Presumably the incident referred to is the death of Head Constable Peter Burke (R.I.C. 62175) on 20 September 1920.
6 Presumably Hugh Massy Lowndes (R.I.C. 55386).

As an instance of the value of some of the evidence given before the Commission here is an excerpt: "Evidence submitted to us by recent members of the Imperial British forces, and corroborated by the testimony of other witnesses, indicates that defection from these forces is frequent, and occasionally is discouraged by killing and flogging of those who too publicly contemplate resigning." It would seem that this groundless allegation pointed to only the R.I.C.

Even the English Labour Commission did not it would appear clearly understand the position of the Black and Tans and Auxiliaries in relation to the R.I.C. They were not recruited for the permanent establishment of the R.I.C. The conditions of their enlistment were entirely different from those of the R.I.C. whose pay was about half that of the Black and Tans, and one fourth that of the Auxiliaries. When the Commission speaks of the *dilution* of these men into the ranks of the R.I.C. the implication would appear to be that the effect was a deterioration of the *morale* of the R.I.C. That would be an entirely erroneous view, as there was no fellowship between the two units. Instead, the R.I.C. detested association with those imports and gave them no assistance beyond accompanying them, when requisitioned, on their raiding expeditions and in these instances were a brake upon their actions instead of assistance.

It was not to do R.I.C. work that those men were employed but work Lloyd George knew the R.I.C. would not do. When his military advisers told him that the rebellion could not be suppressed by police measures Lloyd George did not agree, because he had in view measures by Bandits, something akin to the Baslei Bazooks let loose by Turkey on the Bulgarians in the late 1870s, and of which the voice of the Great Gladstone rang out through the corridors of Europe in memorable denunciation.

The following passage in the report is an instance of how fully the Commission misunderstood the situation:

The insolent and provocative conduct of certain sections of the Crown forces is even more likely to infuse fear or to invite reprisals. In at least one town, to our own knowledge, the R.I.C. often carry Black and Tan flags in their motor lorries, glorying the title which has spread fear throughout the land. Sometimes below it will be found a small Sinn Fein flag, or the flag of the Irish Republic will be trailed in the dust or mire of the road. We would submit that no disciplined force would so deliberately encourage bitterness of spirit or inflame feelings of retaliation in this way.

In another passage the Commission states:

We have witnessed with feelings of shame the insolent swagger of individual Black and Tans in the streets of Irish towns. We have heard raucous voices to the accompaniment of the rumble of the police lorry bawling out the police song:

> "We are the boys of the R.I.C.
> We are as happy as can be."

This is but one instance of many others of the erroneous idea the Commissioners had in reference to the difference between the permanent R.I.C. Force and the temporary Black and Tans and Auxiliaries. Now even their bitterest detractors would not accuse the R.I.C. of behaviour like this. Such conduct and assumption that those off-scourings were members of the R.I.C. was more offensive to them than to the public. Who in this country ever heard of any R.I.C. soul—not to speak of this doggerel—offensively bawled out in rowdylike fashion, to provoke trouble?

Further, at a meeting of the Labour Party called to receive the report of the Commission, Brigadier-General Thomson, military adviser to the Commission, stated in his speech: Turning next to the R.I.C. with which were associated the so-called Black and Tans, he did not suppose that anyone, who was acquainted with the record of the R.I.C. in the past, would care to denounce in general terms that body. They might have had many defects but at least they were men of Irish birth. Unfortunately, a new element has been added to it consisting of Englishmen, Scotchmen and Welshmen. They

were ex-soldiers. They were men habituated to violence in
thought and deed, and he did not think he was exaggerating,
when he said that at least one per cent of them were men of
evil character. Unfortunately, that small fraction had changed
the whole body of the R.I.C. The Black and Tans were men
who would always have the most disagreeable, the most
sinister associations in the minds of the Irish people. They
were the most provocative element in that unhappy country.
He did not suppose that any members of the Commission who
were present at Limerick Junction after they had left Cork,
would forget the scene at that station. There were some
fourteen members of the R.I.C. on the platform, and at least
three of them were under the influence of drink. It was the
most revolting spectacle he had ever seen. These men,
clothed in the uniform which should be the symbol of law and
mercy were behaving like swaggering bullies. They had the
platform at their mercy, because they were armed. He did not
think there was anything that brought home to them whether
Englishmen or Scotchmen the realities of the Irish situation
more clearly than that did, and they (the members of the
Commission) felt ashamed of their country, and they were not
the only cause of the provocation.

Day and night, lorries full of men careering up and down
the main streets of cities and country roads, their occupants
singing or rather shouting,

> "We are the boys of the R.I.C.
> We are as happy as happy can be."

What would the members think if our Constabulary, the men to
whom we applied for help and information, behaved like drunken rowdies returning from a revel? Was that the majesty of the
law (cries of no)? That was the state of things in Ireland today.

Notwithstanding the misconception of both the American
and English Labour Commissions as to the status of the Black
and Tans and Auxiliaries, the report of the English Commission
is a valuable document. The Commission visited the principal

centres of the disturbed areas and took down in writing evidence by reliable people who had personal knowledge of what they stated, and the Commissioners themselves, in the course of their investigations, witnessed the conduct of Black and Tans at railway stations and in the streets of towns, which went to corroborate all they had heard. With this unbiased testimony by English gentlemen, who stated that from what they had seen and heard they were ashamed of their country, their report will be a valuable document for the future historian.

Both Commissions in their reports give testimony of the Black and Tans in their lorry drives, careering wildly along the roads and through the streets of towns, shooting dogs and cattle as they went, and two women outside their own homes. Will anyone, except by general allegations without reliable evidence, try to associate the R.I.C. with those exasperating excursions? Those bandits had nothing to fear from an unarmed helpless people. They could in perfect safety invade towns, masquerade through the streets, print up offensive slogans on public and private buildings, force people to kneel on the streets, curse De Valera and spit on his picture, enter the halls of societies, insult and assault members assembled there, and during their stay, sometimes two or three days, behave generally in a way that should make the blood boil in the veins of any Irishman worthy of the name, and yet there was not a finger raised against them. Where then were the ambushers of the R.I.C. when merely carrying out the ordinary duties of patrolling the country roads in couples? Those patriots, if they did venture on the streets, may have been cuffed and kicked as well as others, as the Black and Tans, in their half drunken behaviour, did not question whether Rebel or Royalist—that he was Irish was sufficient—yet, these bandits came and went without the slightest interference. Even when they went about trailing the Republican flag in the gutter, as described by the English Labour Commission, there was no account of the R.I.C. ambushers. It was only when the soldiers of the revolution, banded in the "Flying Squads" that Lloyd George's Bushi Bazooks were countered with success and only to those

chivalrous young men—not to the ambushers of the R.I.C.—
did Ireland owe the Truce and the end of the conflict.

But while the people rejoiced at the Truce and the prospect
of peace, the type of patriot who engaged in ambushing the
R.I.C. was still in evidence. Recruiting continued for the
Volunteers and Piaras Beaslai in his valuable book states that
many of those men showed themselves far more aggressive
and militant at this time than those who had been through the
previous campaign, and that when the disbandment of the
R.I.C. and Black and Tans commenced these Truce-heroes
took advantage of the occasion to attack them in Kerry and
elsewhere. English military and police lorries unguarded, driven
and occupied by unarmed men, were held up and seized in
many parts of the country. Two British soldiers in a lorry were
shot dead on the Naas road. A British officer was shot dead
on the Crumlin road. These truculent, not to say cowardly
deeds, under the protection of Truce and Treaty reflected only
shame on those responsible, and greatly increased the difficulties of the Provisional Government in dealing with the
English authorities.

Here we have the very type of patriot who engaged in
ambushing the R.I.C. and who now came in at the kill to
have something to chalk up to their credit, just in the same
way as those who, in perfect safety, shot down couples of
unsuspecting R.I.C. An instance exactly similar to those
murders during the Truce was committed at Boyle where
two R.I.C. pensioners, father and son, were taken from their
home and shot because of a lying rumour that they were of
the party who murdered Father Griffin.

That isolated reprisals by the R.I.C took place there can be
little doubt. Piaras Beaslai states that after an attack on
Kilmallock Barracks,[7] in which two Constables were killed and

7 According to both Herlihy, *The Royal Irish Constabulary*, and Abbott,
   Police Casualties in Ireland, the deaths were of a Sergeant Thomas Kane
   (R.I.C. 55093) and a Constable Joseph Morton (R.I.C. 54291). They differ on
   the date of the incident: Herlihy gives it as 29 May 1920 and Abbott a day
   earlier.

five wounded and the barracks burned to the ground, that subsequently the police set fire to several houses, burned a hall, and fired widely through the streets of the town. Another instance, admitted by the Chief Secretary, is given by the English Labour Commission of the burning of creameries at Tubbercurry and Achonry as a reprisal for the murder of a District Inspector and wounding of a Constable in an ambush attack.

But one outstanding instance, next to the murder of Lord Mayor MacCurtain, is that at Thurles which was a strong Republican centre. A District Inspector and Constable were openly shot dead on the public street in broad daylight. Beaslai tells us that Michael Collins had information that most of the R.I.C. in Thurles belonged to the Orange Order, transferred there from the six counties, and that two principal members were a Sergeant known as Captain X and the other as ZY. These police it appears instituted a reign of terror in the town and neighbourhood. People were bullied and beaten daily in the streets and, at night, shooting wildly through the town took place, and two Republicans were shot dead in their beds. From a description of the man who actually shot Thomas MacCurtain, Collins believed firmly that it was this Captain X. About this time, it seems, a murder plot was contemplated to remove noted Republicans and that Captains X and ZY were two of the principals to be employed on the job.

Reference to this murder plot it seems fell into the hands of Collins, in which it was stated that it was useless—mark the word useless—to depend entirely on the R.I.C. for information. A Divisional Commissioner writing stated "I have been told of the new policy and plan, and I am satisfied, though I doubt its ultimate success in the main particular—the stamping out of terror by secret murder."

There may be other instances of reprisals by the R.I.C., but as a body there is no reliable evidence that they had recourse to such methods of revenge for the wanton attacks upon them. The English Labour Commission visited the principal areas of trouble and took statements in writing from various classes of people and, in all those statements, there is not a single allegation against what was known as "The old R.I.C." but, instead, a distinction was made between them and the Black and Tans. The Commission was told of night invasions of dwellings and the shootings of men by men wearing R.I.C. uniform and goggles, but that is not evidence that those murderers were R.I.C. men—rather is it the contrary, for the victims were as a rule people not actively engaged in the Trouble and of which the R.I.C. would have been aware.

That reprisals were chiefly the work of the military and Black and Tans, Beaslai states: "Reprisals became the order of the day, and, after every attack on the Black and Tans and military, houses were burned in the neighbourhood and the nearest town or village shot up. In a number of cases men were taken out and shot as reprisals, the victims being usually persons who had no connection with the Volunteers." Once the R.I.C. vacated outlying small posts consisting of four or five men housed in ordinary buildings—not fortified as represented—and concentrated in larger centres in barracks put into a state of defence, and that they ceased to move about unguardedly, not a single attack was made upon them. It was then they could have taken reprisals with impunity; and, if under any circumstances reprisals were justified, it was in the cowardly attack made on that body. They had not gone out to make an armed attack on the Volunteers but, instead requested to be disarmed as were the Dublin Metropolitan Police. They desired as far as possible not to get mixed up in the Trouble; and, though obliged when required to accompany the Auxiliaries on their raiding expeditions, they were a brake upon rather than helpful in their actions, and the people were glad of their presence on such occasions. An instance of this occurred at Clogheen, County Tipperary, on the night of 21 May 1920. Constable Crowley [presumably R.I.C. 68895] and two other Constables were sent out with two Black and Tans and were ordered by one of the Black and Tans to show them the house of Maurice Walsh and the Chairman of the

Clogheen District Council as he was going to shoot them. The police refused, reminding them that they were not now in the Army. Many other instances similar to the Clogheen affair no doubt happened, but of which the public never heard. Both Auxiliaries and Black and Tans preferred to be without the R.I.C. and went out when and where they wished without them. This Clogheen affair is also an instance showing that the Black and Tans were acting on information received from a source other than the R.I.C.

That the R.I.C was a force of spies, pampered and patted on the back, renegades to their country, and all the rest, is absolutely untrue. During the last forty years of their existence, agrarian and political agitation kept the country in a constant state of ferment. Drink was cheap and added to the trouble with which the police had to contend both in town and country. Duties were heaped upon them which instead of being a labour of love, as their detractors represented, were not only hateful but a physical strain of which the public had little conception. Nothing would have been more pleasing to the men of the Force than to have been relieved of those duties. Conditions in the service were a closed book to the public, who consequently were incapable of forming a just view of the action of its members. Even Piaras Beaslai, whose book bears the impress of truth throughout its comprehensive pages, is much at fault when he states that the R.I.C. had little or nothing to do beyond spying on the people, whom they were trained to hate. The charge of espionage has been made without any evidence beyond John Morley's incidental "eyes and ears" reference, and Mr. Birrell's microscope, which I have dealt with in my book and in these pages.

The statement of Mr Beaslai that the R.I.C. were trained to hate the people from whom they sprung is contrary to fact, as one of the things the men were instructed to do was to cultivate a friendly feeling with the well disposed; and Sir Andrew Reed, the most capable Inspector General that at anytime filled the position, issued a special order on this very matter, directing Country Inspectors not to recommend for promotion any man who was wanting in civility and helpfulness to people making inquiries or in difficulty.

Mr. Beaslai, however, has some redeeming things to say of the Force. He states: "a large number of the R.I.C. notwithstanding their training, had no hostility to their fellow countrymen, and shrunk from a conflict with them. They had drifted into the Force simply as a means of living, and, faced with a clear issue, preferred to stand up with their country to standing up with England." This passage has reference to the flow of resignations at the time. There were he adds, however, some men working for Collins in the R.I.C. whom it was not desirable to allow to resign. A number of these men remained on to the end, acting as intelligence agents for Collins. In another reference to the Black and Tans, Mr Beaslai truly says that "the old R.I.C. who were left in the Force viewed with disgust their compelled association with those off-scourings of rascaldom, who stole one another's money and belongings, who had no code of honour, no scruple, and very little discipline. But they were the right class of men for Sir Hamar Greenwood's job."

The unjustifiable attack on the R.I.C. was the outcome of years of misrepresentation, now industriously circulated more than ever. Yet, the people did not approve, though voiceless at the time. Nor did the soldiers of the revolution, who found in the serving ranks and retired members plenty of useful friends. Michael Collins, Commander in Chief of the Volunteers, did not order or approve of the indiscriminate shooting of the R.I.C. but, instead, got in friendly touch with them and had men in most of the chief centres supplying him with useful information. Those ambushers, as they lay in wait for a patrol of a couple of men to come along and shoot them down, could not see that they were playing into the hands of Lloyd George; for he could point to the savage attacks on the R.I.C. to justify the licence given to the Auxiliaries and Black and Tans to outrage the people, as mere police measures, in the interests of law abiding citizens. But, even if they had been capable of so reasoning, men prepared to carry out cold blooded murderous attacks, as those were, would not be influenced by results, beyond escaping after the deed.

The R.I.C. were placed in a difficult position. They had witnessed the 1916 Rising and the attitude of the people towards it. Even the issue of this revolt was questionable. Young men of short service could resign, without the same concern as married men, or men of long but unpensionable service. They had no guarantee as to their outlook once they resigned; and, if there is one thing more than another to show the difficulty of their position, it is the tragedy of the Civil War.

APPENDIX 1.

EXTRACTS FROM THE R.I.C. SERVICE RECORD FOR THOMAS FENNELL[1]

Number	41310
Age when appointed	18 years
Height	5' 10"
Native county	Londonderry, Antrim
Religion	Catholic
If married, date	16/9/86
Native county of wife	Donegal
Recommendations	S.I. Wray
Trade or calling	Labourer
Appointment on	6 July 75

1   In Jim Herlihy, (1999), *The Royal Irish Constabulary: A Complete Alphabetical List of Officers and Men, 1816–1922* (Dublin: Four Courts, 1999). Thomas Fennell's surname is incorrectly given on p. 146 as Finnell. His service number is cited correctly.

Allocation To which county (in order of Service in each)	Mayo	31/12/75
	Donegal	15/7/83
	King's	1/12/84
	Armagh	25/9/97
	Sligo	10/3/00
Promotions	Acting Sergeant	1/4/85
	Sergeant	1/3/88
	Head Constable	22/9/97
Rewards, Marks of Distinction and Favourable Records	Jub. Rec.	29/6/89
	Commendation	4/4/91
	3rd class favourable record	7 listed
Punishments	None listed	
If Discharged, Dismissed, Resigned, or Dead	Pensioned 7/5/05	

APPENDIX 2.

OBITUARIES 22 MAY 1948

Sligo Independent and West of Ireland Telegraph
EX-HEAD-CONSTABLE FENNELL
The Mall, Sligo.

It was with much regret we noticed the announcement in last
week's issue of the "Sligo Independent", of the death on the
10th instant of Mr. Thomas Fennell, of The Mall, Sligo, one
of the best Head-Constables who ever served in the old Royal
Irish Constabulary, which was known in their day as the best
police force in the world.

Mr. Fennell, who, we believe, was aged 92[1] and a native of
Castledawson, Co. Derry, came to Sligo in 1900 on promotion,[2] and retired from the Force in the early part of the
1914–18 war.[3] He was so efficient in drill, having written a
book on the subject, that he held an important position as a
drill instructor[4] in Britain during the First World War.

He was of a literary bent, and possessed of considerable
intellectual capabilities, which he turned to good account by
his much appreciated articles to popular magazines.

---

1   He was ninety when he died.
2   He was already a Head-Constable when he came to Sligo.
3   He retired in 1905.
4   Most unlikely, given his nationalist sympathies.

At all times he was most unassuming, and of a kindly and sympathetic nature, his charity knew no bounds. The late Mr. Fennell was what was known as a First-class "P Man" in the R.I.C., and during his service in Sligo he displayed remarkable efficiency in connection with his duties, and was held in the highest respect by the general public, officers and men.

His funeral, which was private, took place to the Sligo Cemetery after Solemn Requiem Mass in the Cathedral.

The chief mourners were: Mrs. Fennell (widow); Eugene, Thomas, and Patrick (sons); Sr. M. Peter, Chinese Mission Convent; Mrs. M. J. Murphy, Mrs. M. Finn, Mrs. D. Quaid and Mrs J. Millar (daughters); Mrs T. Fennell (daughter-in-law); M.J. Murphy, M. Finn, D. Quaid and J. Millar (sons-in-law); Desmond, Geraldine and Rosemary Fennell, Patrick, Deirdre, Brian and Grainne Murphy (grandchildren), C. J. O'Connor and J. O'Connor (brothers-in-law).

To his widow, family and friends we extend our sincere sympathy.

Sligo Champion
LATE EX-HEAD CONSTABLE
T. FENNELL, R.I.C.

It was with genuine sorrow that his many friends in Sligo and in various parts of the country learned of the death of ex-Head Const. T. Fennell, R.I.C., which occurred at his residence, The Mall, Sligo. A native of Creagh, Castledawson, Derry, he joined the Royal Irish Constabulary while in his teens and, having served in many parts of Ireland, came to Sligo as Head Constable in 1900.

A man of considerable culture and rare intellectual capabilities, he was a regular contributor to many literary magazines, and his articles were keenly sought by several well-known periodicals. His unassuming nature and high qualities of character won for him the affection and respect of all who knew him and his warm sympathy to anyone in distress will be remembered by many.

His funeral to Sligo Cemetery after Solemn Requiem Mass was private.

The chief mourners were: Mrs. Fennell (widow); Eugene, Thomas, and Patrick (sons); Sr. M. Peter, Chinese Mission Convent; Mrs. M.J. Murphy, Mrs. M. Finn, Mrs. D. Quaid and Mrs J. Millar (daughters); Mrs T. Fennell (daughter-in-law); M.J. Murphy, M. Finn, D. Quaid and J. Millar (sons-in-law); Desmond, Geraldine and Rosemary Fennell, Patrick, Deirdre, Brian and Grainne Murphy (grandchildren), C. J. O'Connor and J. O'Connor (brothers-in-law).